# Survival Meditations for Parents of Teens

for

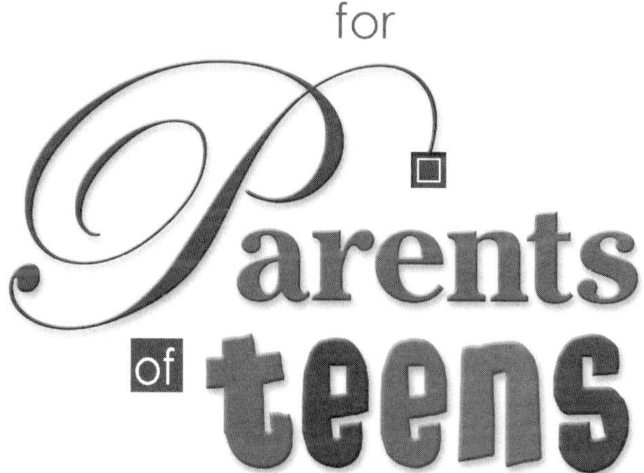


*By Pamela Lowell*

*Illustrations by*
*Lisa Cutri-Mazur*

BOOKS & MEDIA
Boston

**Library of Congress Cataloging-in-Publication Data**

Lowell, Pamela.
Survival meditations for parents of teens / by Pamela Lowell.
p. cm.
ISBN 0-8198-3103-4 (pbk.)
1. Parents—Religious life. 2. Parenting—Religious aspects—Christianity. 3. Parent and teenager—Religious aspects—Christianity. I. Title.
BV4529.L69 2004
242'.645--dc22

2003021638

ISBN 0-8198-3103-4



Printed and published in the U.S.A. by Pauline Books & Media, 50 Saint Pauls Avenue, Boston, MA 02130-3491.

www.pauline.org

Pauline Books & Media is the publishing house of the Daughters of St. Paul, an international congregation of women religious serving the Church with the communications media.

1 2 3 4 5 6 7 10 09 08 07 06 05 04

*For all parents of teenagers:*
*God bless us on this journey.*

# Contents

# Preface

Although I've given counseling advice to families with teenagers for over twenty years, parenting my own teenager has been the most humbling experience I've ever encountered, bar none. Many times during the preparation of this manuscript, I felt as if I were the *last* person in the world who should be offering spiritual advice on such a difficult topic! Despite my professional training, our family is *far* from perfect; we worry, we argue, we bump up against each other's vulnerabilities, and then we apologize—*all the time*.

In fact, during the early months of my son's teenager-hood, I would often sit at my computer, typing furiously, trying to make sense of all of the changes that he and I were going through. There on the screen, I would vent my anxieties and anger and grief, and then after each entry, I would try to write something hopeful, something God-*full*, to help me to keep going, to try to survive. One day, when it finally seemed we were entering a new and better phase, I wondered if anyone else could benefit from my experiences. As it turned out, perhaps they could.

This book would have been impossible to write based solely on my own parenting however, and I wouldn't dream of exposing my teens in that way! I needed to draw from a broader depth of knowledge and experience. So, as friends, neighbors, and parents in my community learned what I was writing about, they voluntarily and courageously shared their stories with *me*.

In addition, throughout the years I have read professional books, done coursework, had cases, supervision, and teachers—as well as spiritual direction—that have all helped to shape my views on parenting. I have quoted from these resources when appropriate, and a source-list appears at the end of the book.

A combination of vignettes from friends, neighbors, family members, and my own clinical work make up the main body of this book. None of the anecdotes are written exactly as they happened in real life. No names or identifying information is used in an effort to protect confidentiality.

*God Help Me!* was a personal cry, born of painful moments when I felt so all alone—as most of us do at times when we are parenting our teens. It is a simple book, about coming out of the shadows and sharing our parenting stories with each other. But mostly it is about surviving our child's adolescence with spirit and faith. If the stories and meditations seem familiar, they are; they are universal, transcending time and place, because ultimately, the stories come from God.

# Acknowledgments

A special thank you to:

Rev. John Morgan, whose book, *Awakening the Soul,* awakened mine; his generous spirit allowed me to use a similar format for this work.

Lisa B., Lynn B., Vicki C., Lisa M., Jean B., Georgeann M., and Nancy B., who openly shared their experiences of parenting teens. And to the many families I've worked with over the years who have blessed me with the honor of hearing their stories.

The wonderful staff at Pauline Books & Media, who were enthusiastic and committed from the very start of this project, and especially to Molly Rosa, my editor, whose loving hand helped to make these entries ring clear and true.

My community of parents, including all of the parents of Barrington Cares, who share the journey and have their own stories to tell. And to old, dear friends (and parents themselves): Ellyn and Ric, Anne M., Dawn and Bob, Sue F., Nancy and Steve, Mary and Steve, Jan and George, and all the rest.

My spiritual director, Judy, who confirms my faith and keeps me on the path: there are no words.

My mother, and my sisters Amy and Jill, and in memory of Dad, who shared my own teenage journey.

My husband, Mark, who allows my soul to flourish always, and who teaches me every day how to be a better parent—I am so grateful.

And finally, to my two sons, Edmund and Warren, whom I love and cherish with all my heart.

# January

Off to a New Year. A fresh start.

Maybe this year will be better than last. To be sure, it will be *different*. How can I keep that feeling of hopefulness about me during times when I am pushed to the edge?

I will resolve to take care of my needs better this year, and not look to my child to fill them. Every day I will set aside time for myself: a walk, a special treat, or a phone call to a friend.

*Holy Creator, help me to embrace this new year, and to look each day for the positive moments, however small and fleeting they may sometimes be.*

## *January 2*

We had another battle yesterday. The day was progressing so peacefully, yet it fell apart so quickly. We both said things we shouldn't have, but afterward, when I went to hug him, he pulled away. Where is the baby I once rocked to sleep every night?

I must remember that the baby is still there, but now a new face is emerging, needing love and guidance, but also independence.

*Loving God, help me to put aside my need for reassurance for now, knowing that someday he will again open his arms for me.*

"We're going to John's and then Allie's and then Christian's, but first we're going to need a ride to the movies... Oh, and I need some money, because Allie forgot hers."

Me, me, me! That's all my teen seems to care about. It's as if she thinks the universe has been created just for her.

This self-centeredness is part of a phase; she is trying to establish a new identity, though awkwardly at times. Being self-centered is how my teen tends to relate to others right now, but perhaps I can move her toward considering my feelings too, especially if I remind her gently, when she's not with her many friends.

*Generous Lord, help me teach her, in my unselfishness, how to be a giving adult in this sometimes un-giving world.*

It's often colder inside our house than it is outside. Sometimes she looks at me with such anger! She can explode over the tiniest thing, then she freezes me out—it's so unpredictable. It's as if a stranger has entered her body, and the real daughter I once knew is never coming back.

I must recognize that she's in the midst of growing into a teenager, with all the fluctuating moods and emotions that come with that time. Angry outbursts and moodiness are normal, as long as periods of relative calm follow those turbulent times. When we have both calmed down, I need to tell her how her anger affects me.

*Help me, God, through this winter of her coldness. Let me be a forgiving hearth where she can warm herself once the anger subsides.*

It's difficult to balance all the needs that I feel constantly pulling at me, to take care of my spouse, my children, obligations to work and family, church and community. When I take time out for myself, it feels wrong—*selfish* somehow.

It's not selfish. It's self-*care.* We can't offer water to others when our own well is dry. *Self-care* is filling the well. Self-care is exercising, eating, and sleeping in healthy ways. It's also solitary time, time for play and laughter, and time for prayer.

*Selfish* is not taking care of our own needs and expecting others to fill them. The pursuit of material and other interests can be selfish, too, if it is used to avoid or replace our loved ones.

*Jesus, Bread of Life, help me find ways to take care of myself during this demanding time of my life so that I will have more than enough to nourish my family and those around me.*

Last night we had the best conversation in months.

Mostly, I just listened. It ended with a rare hug.

At this stage what we *don't* say can sometimes be more important than what we *do*. Teens can start by telling us something outlandish, only to correct their own crazy thinking—by themselves—if we don't jump in and interfere.

*O God, help me listen to her patiently, so that she can form good and healthy opinions, just as you are always there in your infinite wisdom to listen to me.*

"Why, O LORD, do you stand far off?
Why do you hide yourself in times of trouble?"

*Psalm 10:1*

Sometimes we feel so alone during our child's adolescence, as if everyone has abandoned us, even God. It takes so much energy to stay on top of things. We sometimes feel such anger, frustration, and grief. Yet, God is with us during these times—we need only to ask for help.

*Come closer to me, dear Lord, and guide me. I need to hear you telling me again and again,* "I am with you. I am with you, always."

My daughter refuses to continue her dance class, an activity that I think she *should* continue. I lecture, I reason, but still she refuses—and is confident about her decision. I'm angry she's quitting not simply because she is so good at it, but also because I guess I took a certain pride in her achievements.

My daughter's needs and interests are shifting. What once gave her a sense of pleasure and satisfaction, may not now. She needs to follow her own dreams, but I have a right to question her, to make sure that she completely understands the consequences of her decisions.

*God, please help her to know what is right for her. Help me let go of my desire to make all of the decisions for my teen, and to trust that you will be there to help guide her when we sometimes disagree. We are all in your capable hands.*

"All you do is get mad at me! You think everything I do is wrong!"

Who speaks these words?

Sometimes it's my teen; sometimes it's me.

*Help me, loving God, to notice all the good things my teen does, and to tell him so. There will be times when I find myself starting to correct him, but for every time I suggest another way of doing things or find myself getting angry, let me find ten things that I can praise about him, too. Help me to be a safe harbor where he can sometimes rest, free from criticism, as you, my God, are that safe harbor for me.*

She broke one of our rules last night. She went to another place without letting me know she had left the first, and I couldn't get in touch with her. I was worried, angry, and disappointed, so I grounded her. "You're so unfair!" she screamed, as she went stomping up to her room.

The more she pulls away, the tighter I want to grasp. So much in this world is dangerous and unknown. She needs to be able to make some mistakes within the safety net of home. I know that I must allow her to experience freedom, but within certain guidelines. It's not too much to expect her to inform me of changing plans along the way.

*Holy Spirit, please guide my teen and me when either of us strays off the path.*

"None of my friends have to do that! You're the strictest parent in the whole school!"

Is that true? Sometimes I'm so busy with chores and obligations that I become disconnected from my community of other parents.

I need to take the time to make that phone call for connection and clarification. It is my business to know the rules and values held by the parents of my children's friends, since my teen is spending time with them. Connected by a myriad of relationships, we are all a part of something bigger, with responsibility to each other.

*God, you watch over all of us with loving concern, as is fitting of our Heavenly Father. Please show me your face in the faces of my community. Guide me to connect with them in love and understanding. We are all your children.*

"Few of us are aware of how close we are with our children, until we lose them to adolescence."

*Michael J. Bradley, Ph.D.*

Something is different. Everything is changing so fast. A part of me wants to turn the clock back and freeze time. I yearn for that physical affection, that previous adulation from my child, but it's not to be, and the pain of it sears through my heart like a knife.

We must first mourn the very real loss of a relationship with our loving, complacent child before we can move on to accept the wonderful teen, who is in the process of becoming an adult.

*O Mary, you who have grieved so much, help me to grieve the loss of my "little one." Help me to welcome my new child, the wonderful adolescent who is growing into a wonderful adult.*

I linger outside her room for a few minutes while she is talking on the phone, overhearing something I wish I hadn't. It wasn't necessarily a bad thing, but probably none of my business just the same. She never talks to me anymore, not like she used to. Who is this secret self?

She needs to separate from me in order to form a new identity, one that is hers alone. She will take the best from me, but will experiment and try on different faces as she figures out who she wants to be.

*Help me, dear God, to remember that she is on a journey of self-discovery, which will include some private moments before she can willingly share more of her new self with me.*

She doesn't seem to be hanging out with the same friends anymore. One girl seemed so sweet, but when I asked her about that friend, she told me that I just didn't understand, and refused to give me any more details. Lately, she's spending a lot of time alone.

Teens will intuitively move away from peers that make them feel uncomfortable, or whose morals or values conflict with theirs, or who are at a different developmental stage. It's important for them to be able to choose their own friends—we can't do it for them. Yet, it's normal for us to feel helpless at times as we watch our children struggle with all the complex and sometimes-painful issues of "friendship."

*Jesus, help her to discern well who her friends will be, just as you gathered your Apostles to help support you and spread your words of love. Guide her as she seeks out true friends, those who will love and honor her authentic self. With your help and guidance, she will create a circle of trustworthy companions.*

My son seems so unmotivated these days. Other teenagers seem to be out accomplishing so much. He wants to spend his time on the computer or listening to music or just hanging out with friends. I'm afraid he's not going to amount to anything! A part of me is jealous of the parents of those over-achieving children.

It's so difficult to balance our expectations with our children's needs and desires. How much to push? How much to let happen by itself?

*All-knowing God, help me to be patient as together we guide this child into adulthood. Help me to put aside my jealousy of those over-achieving children, knowing that my teen's desire to succeed must come not from me, but from within himself in order to burn bright and true. Help me to trust that with your love and tender guidance, he will become all he is meant to be.*

We have gone several days now without an argument.

It feels like the old child I knew is back again.

Every step our teens take toward us will be accompanied by two steps farther away. This is right and true.

*Help me, O God, to remain open to all that this process of change is unfolding. Don't let me hold on too tightly, or anticipate too soon that the most challenging times are over. Remind me that my teen is in your capable hands as he comes to know himself and this world.*

When she flips on the radio in the car, I want to scream. I don't like her music, it's loud, annoying, and it doesn't make sense. I feel so old, used up, and out of touch. I don't like feeling this way.

How can I manage not to judge her taste, but instead to talk with her about the specifics? Can I ask: Who wrote the song? Do other kids like it? Do they play it at dances?

We need to talk about music in order to connect, remembering that parents aren't *supposed* to like teenagers' music. The function of teenage music is to define and separate from the generation that came before.

*O God, you create each of us as special and unique. Help me to accept the ways in which my teen is defining herself as uniquely different from me through her taste in music, as well as other things.*

My son is constantly online with his friends. It is how they stay connected and make plans in this cyber-world. He has over one hundred "buddies" on his buddy list. Who are all those people? They all exchange ideas and plans in this super-charged, super-technological society.

I need to keep up-to-date with his world, even if it is so confusing!

*Lord, you who know all things, help me to understand the appeal and dangers of this ever-changing technology, so that I can help him stay safely connected to others–and to our values here at home.*

I woke up this morning and decided to go skating on the pond by the stone house. No one wanted to go with me, so I went by myself. The pond's face was wet and wrinkled in some places, like my own. I had been feeling stressed all week, but something happened this morning when I skated alone; a crack widened deep inside me, and something untied. When I got home, I felt refreshed and renewed, and closer to God.

When is the last time I defined and replenished a need of my spirit?

*Holy Spirit, help me to be a model for my children of how to fulfill the regular need for solitude, prayer, and spiritual replenishment.*

Yesterday my daughter spent over an hour organizing her stuffed animals on her bed—then hurried to get ready for her first date. She's fifteen, with one foot still in childhood and the other out the door. So many tears and disappointments lie ahead, but such joy, too. She's ever changing, this little girl/woman whom I once knew so well. Who is she from moment to moment?

I remember how difficult those years were for me, not knowing all the answers. It is a time of questions and self-doubt, a roller coaster of emotions, with a strong push to leave and an equally strong pull to stay.

*Holy Mary, Mother of God, help me to love equally the girl she still is and the woman she is in the process of becoming. Although at times things between us may be a bit rocky, let our relationship evolve as she grows, so that I can be there for her in every stage of her development: loving her, cherishing her, and supporting her throughout her life.*

We had a long talk with our daughters yesterday about getting along better with one another. They aired their grievances, each taking responsibility for their part. After weeks of bickering, the oldest was so kind to her younger sister today, combing her hair, and sharing a favorite magazine. The youngest was more kind, less annoying, and more her true self. They played together for hours, discovering each other again, like old friends.

If they acknowledge the part that they *both* play in getting along, it will help, especially if I don't blame one or the other when things aren't going right.

*Show me, dear Lord, when to intervene so that my children may learn the important skills of communication and compromise, and when to let them resolve things for themselves.*

I found out that the boy-girl party my daughter went to last weekend was unsupervised most of the time. I feel sick! What if something terrible had happened? What were those parents thinking! I'm so angry that they would think this was okay. I called another girl's mother to see what she thought about it, and she was shocked! We agreed never to let our daughters go to a party there again.

It is easy when we are feeling so angry and betrayed to seek out others who might feel the same way. To gossip about and isolate parents who put our children at risk essentially avoids a discussion with the very people with whom we *should* be sharing our concerns. It takes courage to approach another parent in this situation, but it may be the only time someone has cared enough to acknowledge the problem and offer possible solutions and compromise.

*Jesus, you have taught us the important lesson of loving our neighbor. Help me to move away from judgment and condemnation toward dialogue and forgiveness. Help us to find a way to reach some middle ground, so that all of our children will be watched over and safe.*

"When you get into a tight place, and everything goes against you, 'til it seems as if you couldn't hold on a minute longer, never give up then, for that's just the place and time that the *tide'll turn.*"

*Harriet Beecher Stowe*

When am I feeling most helpless and depleted in dealing with my teen? How do I handle those feelings of hopelessness? Sometimes it feels as if my relationship with my teen has reached the lowest possible place. It takes faith, hope, and prayer to turn the tide to a place of deeper love and understanding.

*God, please give me all the courage I need not to give up when things seem most difficult. Help me hang on when I need it the most, in the faith that with the grace of your love* "the tide *will* turn."

He is finding his way in the world, outside my sphere of influence. Some of his friends are from races and religions so different from our family. Some of his friend's families have more money than our family does—others are much poorer. He likes them all, but, at times, I find myself passing judgment on people or things that aren't familiar to me.

We are all so much more alike than different, each of us striving to do our best in a world filled with diversity and confusion. It is good that he wants to explore what is different, so that he will better understand the world he will one day navigate on his own.

*Loving Christ, soften my heart. Help me be grateful for the gift of my tolerant teen, who teaches me through you how to be more loving and accepting of those who are different from me.*

Whose voice is deepening? Whose body has curves? Sexuality has *never* been something I have felt comfortable talking about. My parents never talked to me!

I need to recognize that my child is growing and developing sexually, and with this development emerges questions, needs, and desires. She needs to know my values, as there will be much in the world to contradict what our faith teaches us. I must fight through my embarrassment about this topic, so that we can discuss it in ways that help her feel normal and healthy, and keep her safe.

*Holy Spirit, you who delight in our every stage of growth and development, show me how to guide my teen through these sometimes awkward stages.*

Today I called a parent I didn't know to check about a ride to the movies for my daughter and her new boyfriend. What a strange feeling! I felt so nervous about calling. Our children are connected, but we have never met. My daughter was mortified. "*Why can't you trust me?*" she cried, wanting to make all the arrangements herself.

Surprise! The other parent was relieved and grateful that I called because her son had "forbidden" her to call me! We talked for a while, agreeing on some ground rules for their relationship, promising to always have adult supervision when they spend time together in our homes. She thanked me again for calling, saying she felt like she could count on my support.

*Let me remember, dear God, that there may be times when someone needs me to reach into their life for connection and reassurance, just as you reach into my life to comfort and reassure me.*

**Parent-to-parent connection** 

Sometimes she "forgets" to take the dog out when she comes home from school—something she has promised to do. The poor animal has to wait until I get home from work, and I often have to clean up his messes. It makes me angry that she's avoiding this important chore, but it's too much trouble and I'm too tired most of the time to enforce the rules.

But she needs to know that there will be consequences and rewards for her behavior at home, in order to be more prepared for the real world. When she leaves us someday, she needs to have learned that her actions have an impact on others, and that her unwillingness to act has consequences, too.

*Heavenly Father, in his life here on earth, Jesus clearly defined our duty toward you, and showed us the path to your glory. God, help me hold my teen to her obligations instead of rescuing her from her chores and duties, so that she will develop into a more responsible and loving adult. In this way, she will move ever closer to your glory.*

Last night a parent shared some nasty gossip with me about one of my son's friends. I didn't try to change the subject or redirect her words. I could have said, "*I feel uncomfortable. I wouldn't want you to think I would talk about your child when you weren't around,*" but I didn't. A part of me wanted to hear more of what she had to say.

Although we sometimes need to share information as parents, gossip is a destructive force, pervasive and wrong. It takes moral courage to stand up to gossip. It takes reaching away from isolation and toward community; away from separateness and toward inclusion.

*Jesus, Light of the World, guide me as I try to reach for the light of my finer self. Help me not to gossip, or to judge or condemn those who do, but to recognize that with your help I can light the way for others–by only speaking words that are kind and true.*

On the drive home today, I overheard my son talking to his friend about a problem another friend is going through. My son was caring and compassionate, really listening. As I was telling my husband how proud I was, he replied, "That's great! Did you tell *him* how proud you felt?" And I had to admit that I hadn't even thought of it.

When I told my son how proud I was to hear him relating to one of his friends in such a positive way, he beamed. Yes, of course he beamed. Why couldn't I have figured that out myself? Why is it sometimes easier for me to chastise my child when he does something wrong than to applaud him for doing something right?

*Help me, Lord, to notice your face in his–and remind me to tell him so.*

"Weeping may linger for the night,
but joy comes with the morning."

*Psalm 30:5*

Suddenly she's no longer "daddy's girl." She pushes her father away with a vengeance! All those hours spent with her years ago, a soft fuzzy baby curled up in his lap, and now she doesn't even want him to touch her. This is agony for him! He can hardly bear this loss. He avoids her, saying his heart is retreating, protecting itself, not knowing how to connect with this stranger who now stands before him.

*Blessed God, hold my husband in his sorrow. Comfort him in his loss. Help him to find new ways to reach out to her again, trusting that she needs and loves him, even when she's pushing him away.*

Yesterday, she told a funny joke at dinner. It was witty and clever, not like the biting sarcasm she has used in the recent past. We laughed until we cried. It was good to laugh together again.

Humor is a wonderful connecting point. Laughter helps to get us through the rough spots. During our darkest hours, it helps to have a sense of humor.

*Dear Lord, help me to see the humor in raising an adolescent. And help me to feel you, O God, smiling knowingly by my side.*

# February

Last night my friend's son had another argument with his girlfriend. My friend woke up and heard her son shouting on the phone at two in the morning. He was so tired when he got up for school this morning. Later, she noticed a hole in the wall of his room. It scared her. And it reminded her of the times when she or her husband have hit or thrown something in anger.

How do we handle our strong emotions? Are we teaching through our actions that it's okay to be destructive or violent when angry? We all get angry sometimes. It's important to talk with our teens about how they control their anger. But we also need to control ourselves when we're upset, so we can learn how to deal with issues in a more peaceful way.

*Passionate God, hear our prayer. Our out-of-control anger hurts the very people we love with all our heart. Fill us with your patience, love, and understanding. Heal our brokenness.*

Groundhog Day. How much longer will my relationship with my teen remain in winter's grasp: dark, disagreeable, dismal? How I wish he could just pop out of a little dirt-hole with a smile on his face—an announcement of spring!

*Jesus, Light of the World, please remind me that even in the darkness there is hope for renewal. As my teen changes, I, too, will need to grow and change. The days will become longer and brighter. When our springtime comes, we will smile again.*

Her boyfriend acts strangely jealous when she goes out with her other friends. He wants her to quit her part-time job so she can be with him all the time. He tells her she is the only one who understands his moody outbursts.

These are the early signs of an abusive relationship. Controlling, jealous behavior tends to become worse over time, sometimes resulting in physical violence. Do I know how to warn my daughter before she gets in over her head? Does she know how to assert her needs in a relationship? Does she know how to leave a relationship without fear of repercussion?

*All-protective God, assist me in seeking guidance and intervention quickly, as she may not know how to protect herself, and I may not fully know how to help her.*

"Anger is basically a matter of choice. It is determined by your thoughts and beliefs far more than your biochemistry or genetic heritage."

*Matthew McKay, Ph.D.*

What "shoulds" am I telling myself about a situation that causes my anger to flare? When do I choose to express my anger? When do I hold myself back? Are there patterns to my anger? Am I angrier when I am overstressed, hungry, sick, or tired? Do I have a plan for how to deal with the people or situations that trigger my anger-response? Do I know how and when it's appropriate to express my anger?

I need to learn more about my anger, which is neither good nor bad, but more like my body's way of sending me information that someone or something has violated my boundaries.

*Jesus, my Savior, you knew the value of expressing anger appropriately. Didn't you become angry with the moneylenders in the temple? Please teach me about the emotion of anger. Help me also to prevent my inappropriately angry responses by taking better care of myself, by spending time with you in prayer and solitude, and by expressing my needs when I am calm and able to think clearly.*

She refuses to go to counseling to help her with her abusive relationship with this boy. Last night she came home with a bruise on the side of her face, saying the car door "accidentally" hit her. I'm at my wit's end, trying to convince her to get help!

If I sense my child is in imminent danger, then I *must* get professional help. Maybe I can go to counseling alone the first time, or ask my daughter if she wants to bring a friend. I need to do *anything* to begin the process of intervention, which will lead to her eventual healing.

*Healing God, help us with this enormous problem, which seems almost insurmountable to me. I'm so frightened for her, and the way is unclear. I need to rely on your Divine Providence to help guide us in the right direction.*

Yesterday, during an argument, my son cursed at me, called me terrible names. I cursed back and slapped him across the face. He ran from the room, crying. I feel awful! I've lost my temper before, but never, *ever*, like this. Although I apologized, there is a great distance between us now and I wonder if we will ever feel close again.

I must take the steps necessary to insure that it *never* happens again. My son was wrong to talk to me the way he did, but violence is never a solution. So much self-doubt and recrimination; I can't stop replaying the scene over in my mind. But through it all, I am trying to remember: if God can forgive me, perhaps I can forgive myself. And someday, perhaps, my son will forgive me, too.

*Jesus, you who forgave those who did you the most harm, please guide me and my child in the ways of forgiveness. I am so deeply sorry for what I have done.*

***February 7***

"And he woke up and rebuked the wind and the raging waves, they ceased, and there was calm."

*Luke 8:24*

To stay calm in the storm of his adolescence, that is a worthy goal. I need to calmly tell him my expectations, so that he can better reflect on his own behavior, and on *what* I said, instead of focusing on *how* I said it.

*O Heavenly Father, in your magnificent benevolence, thank you for showing me what it means to be a loving and accepting parent.*

Sometimes, right after she wakes up, I can tell we're going to have a bad day. She says she's not a "morning" person, but I know she didn't get to bed until late last night. I sense that her days have become too busy.

How can I help my daughter establish good routines? She needs to get enough sleep, possibly eight or nine hours every night. She shouldn't get over stimulated right before bedtime by talking on the phone or e-mailing friends. Her activities must be managed and balanced, and she should have plenty of room for downtime and fun! I need to teach her how to take care of herself, and I need to model that behavior by taking especially good care of myself.

*Thank you, O God, for my teen's mind, body, and soul. Help her to know that she is your marvelous creation, made in your image and likeness, and worth taking care of.*

My friend should have left her husband a long time ago—all the bruises, the lies, and the pain. She's been afraid to leave, believing what he says: that she won't be able to make it on her own. She makes excuses for his behavior, saying he brings in a good income to support them. But even she has to admit that his violent moods are starting to affect the children. She's at the end of her rope and he refuses to go for counseling. I tell her that he's wrong to be treating her this way, and that the time to leave is *now*. But what if she can't survive? I just hope I'm saying the right thing.

Children deserve to be loved and cherished by parents who exhibit loving behavior toward each other. Abused spouses need to find the strength to see all of their options clearly, and to do what is right so that they can be safe from harm. Sometimes a friend's validation will give them the strength they need to leave an unhealthy, dangerous relationship.

*Heavenly Father, my friend is so desperate and so very afraid. Guide her in your will. This is too big of a problem to handle by herself. Please help her, through others, to find a way toward peace and safety. Please help me know the right words to lend direction and to be of comfort to my friend.*

A girl keeps calling and asking to speak to my son. He takes the call in private, and doesn't mention her name. She sounds cute and polite on the phone; still I feel a twinge of worry. He's only in middle school!

It's normal for parents to feel some hesitation when their children become interested in the opposite sex—or the opposite sex become interested in them! It's important to realize that most of these early "crushes" are short-lived—especially if we don't overreact—and are part of normal development in the life of our teen.

*O God, please guard me against my over-protective tendencies. Let me be open and welcoming to the new relationships that will come into my family. Help me to see that by embracing others our lives will become enriched and expanded, moving us toward the future, and ultimately, closer to you.*

"No one will ever love me!"

During those gawky, teenage years, it may seem as if true love will never be found. Dating? Companionship? Marriage? Girls start to think and dream about such things during this time; boys do, too—even though it will be many more years before these dreams come true. What can help sustain my teen during the lonely times ahead?

Whenever I am feeling unloved or lonely, it always helps to remind myself that God is passionately in love with me. God is crazy about me! It's true! How can I impart this important lesson to my teen?

*Help me show them all the ways that you love me, O God, so that during those inevitable times of loneliness and doubt, my teen will always feel the sustaining warmth of your embrace.*

His heart is broken. The girl he's been seeing for over a year has dumped him without warning in his senior year of high school. I've never seen him so sad. He stares into space, glumly, telling me he's lost his best friend. I can see it's for the best, but I'm worried about him, too.

For adolescents, a break-up can be devastating, at least temporarily. It's difficult for them to imagine ever recovering, or loving anyone else ever again. They need time and space to grieve, but if those feelings continue after two weeks or so, it may be a signal that something else needs attention.

*O God, help me to understand my child's hurt during this time. Please be there for him as he struggles through the pain of a lost love, and give him the courage to love again one day.*

## *February 13*

This morning, the trees were glistening with ice from a powerful storm last night. Every branch, every twig, had a perfectly formed droplet of ice, and the sun was brilliant in every crystal. It seemed as though God was everywhere this morning. I could see God *everywhere.*

When we take time to contemplate nature, it's easy to find God in its beauty.

*Magnificent God, allow me to find your presence in all things–in the extraordinary as well as the tiny miracles, which you alone provide. Help me bring your glory into my home, into my family, into my teen, into my life.* Every *day.*

She's made Valentines for all her friends, but apparently, she has a secret "crush" on one particular boy. She's hoping he will notice her and ask her to the dance. But he's one of those "popular" boys, one who seems to have a different girlfriend every week. I want to say something, because I'm so afraid she'll only end up getting hurt, but it's so hard to know what to say!

The arena of teenage "love" and "crushes" is very delicate. As parents, we need to find the right words to say, to know when to *stop* saying them, and to be available when there are no more words to say. Asking open-ended questions, which can help a teen to figure out his or her feelings, while reserving judgment and advice is usually the best way to handle this situation.

*O God, I can feel your powerful presence, especially when I am quiet and still; and the need for words, any words, all but disappears. Help me to be a powerfully still and comforting presence for my delicate young teen.*

## *February 15*

I'm worried about her relationship with one boy. He doesn't seem to care about her, doesn't return her calls, and ignores her at school. Last night I told her, "Be careful not to give your heart to someone who will treat it so casually. Your heart is valuable, and it deserves tender care."

She got angry with me, saying, "What are you talking about? He's not like that at all!"

I must be careful not to jump in too fast! She probably knows that something is wrong, but isn't ready to admit it yet. I can't protect her from all the little heartaches in this world—no matter how hard I try. She will need to learn some things for herself, even if that means experiencing a broken heart.

*Loving God, show me the way to support her without being intrusive or presumptuous, as you support me all the days of my life.*

She kept her room spotlessly clean for an entire week! When I told her how pleased I was, she shrugged it off as if it meant nothing to her, but then, out of the corner of my eye, I saw she was beaming.

For all the bravado, a place inside her wants so much to please me. I must remember to praise, praise, praise—even the little things. Little things are the stuff of relationships. Paying attention to the little things is so important in the life of our teens.

*Help me, O God, to notice the little things.*

### *February 17*

"Relationships are like lawns, we need to water them—whether they look like they need it or not."

*Anonymous*

My spouse and I went out to dinner last night, without the kids. What a strange sensation! We promised each other we wouldn't spend all of our time talking about *them.* So we laughed and talked about our hopes and dreams and sometimes about nothing at all, just like two old souls who've been apart for a long time. It was wonderful.

I need to remember to nourish my adult relationships, whether they look like they need it or not.

*I am so grateful, dear Lord, for your gift of loving companions on this our earthly journey.*

My elderly father called today to report on his weekly trip to the doctor. As he rambled on about his health, I found myself growing impatient, not wanting to listen, and not wanting to face the fact that he's growing old. And then I guiltily rushed him off the phone; I had a million other things to do.

How difficult it is to have patience with our aging parents. In our struggle to balance everyone's needs, they can sometimes feel like just another inconvenient burden. In addition to our time-consuming teenagers, we suddenly find ourselves having to take care of our parent's changing needs as well. It doesn't feel as though we have the energy for it all, which is why it's vitally important to make sure that we replenish ourselves during this very busy and ever-giving time of life.

*Jesus, you who were lovingly devoted to Mary and Joseph, remind us to honor our parents. Please help me to reach across to the generations on either side of me as you do: with love, compassion, and kindness.*

"Do not fear, for I am with you,
do not be afraid, for I am your God."

*Isaiah 41:10*

Life can be overwhelming when you are the parent of a teenager. Sometimes God feels very distant, especially when I am too busy, stressed, worried, or anxious.

When is the last time I centered myself on God? When have I last been still enough to hear the word of God?

*Help me be still, O God, so I may find myself moving far away from worry, and instead, moving toward the ultimately calming presence of you.*

This morning our son said he didn't want to go to church. He told us he had a term project due for school, but lately he's been avoiding going with us, using all sorts of excuses. He's almost eighteen. We don't want to constantly pressure him into attending services, but it worries us that he seems to be turning his back on his faith.

Have there been times in our lives when we've been lost? How did we find our way? It's normal for teenagers to begin to struggle with and question their faith; the teenage years are a time of great internal searching. After we have taught them about faith and guided them to this point in life, sometimes we can only pray that they find their way home to God.

*Jesus, Good Shepherd, please watch over one of your flock. Please walk with him on this difficult and lonely journey as he struggles with his faith. I pray that my son, your lost and gentle lamb, will find his way back to you.*

"Even Jesus was weary from the journey: He sat down by the well of life, too tired to go on with his apostles, and he asked for refreshment."

*Joyce Rupp*

Raising an adolescent is an incredible task, a monumental journey, where we will learn much about ourselves, but also feel depleted much of the time. Raising a teen is not a short walk in the park; it's more like hiking the whole Appalachian Trail! We need to remember to pace ourselves, and rest along the way.

*Help me, Jesus, Water of Life, to recognize when I am depleted. Restore and nourish me on this journey of life.*

This afternoon I took some much-needed time off from work. At first, I thought about all the chores I had waiting, all the errands to run, and all the bills that needed to be paid. Then, feeling exhausted before I began, I stopped and didn't do anything at all. I just rested—the entire afternoon. When I told my son, rather guiltily, what had happened, he said, "But you did do something. You took care of yourself."

*God of refreshing love, remind me to take time away from this over-scheduled world. Help me to be still sometimes, and to remember always that I am your beloved, your precious one, deserving of rest.*

At dinner last night, we realized we hadn't eaten a meal together in over a week, because of John's basketball practice, Monica's rehearsal, my husband's business trip, and my being tied up with getting everyone where they needed to go. How did we allow this to happen? Why in the world are we letting activities get in the way of being together?

Families that regularly share meals together have the largest percentage of teenagers who don't engage in self-destructive behavior. What activities are keeping us apart? Is this a temporary situation due to a time-limited commitment, or a permanent habit?

*All-knowing God, help us to make time for each other away from our activities, so that we can celebrate our "family-ness" together. It is in this quiet celebration of family that we find ourselves coming closer to you.*

His room has become a disaster! There's food everywhere, dirty dishes, laundry strewn about! But even when he does finally clean up, it just doesn't stay that way. We've been having so many arguments lately. He used to be such a neat and tidy child.

An adolescent's external world tends to mirror his inner world. Everything about him is growing, shifting, changing. His body, his voice, the way he thinks and feels are all in disarray. When the internal changes begin to settle down—maybe in several years!—so will the way he orders his life. Sometimes, it is best to just close the door to his room and not look in for a while!

*Holy Spirit, give me patience with life's little messes.*

**Caution: messy rooms ahead** 

My fourteen-year-old son wants to get his eyebrow pierced. My daughter wants a tattoo. They tell me all the other kids are doing these things, but it still feels so wrong to me.

An adolescent's world is immediate. Rarely do they think about the long-term (and sometimes irreversible) consequences of their actions. It's up to me as a parent to allow the conversation and share my concerns, while setting limits on what I believe are harmful activities. When they become adults, then they can make their own decisions.

*Dear Father, help me stay strong and wise in my convictions, and not let society dictate what is best for my teen.*

Last night I sat and listened as she practiced a difficult piece of music. She stumbled, then corrected herself, stumbled, and then corrected herself again. She did this repeatedly, until she got it right. It was beautiful!

Growing up is like that, stopping and starting, not always fluid, in harmony only part of the time.

*God of all creation, help me listen hard for my child's unique "melody," her unique gift, so that I don't miss it when it bursts forth into the world, like the glorious notes of a song.*

"All things are difficult before they are easy."

*Matthew Henry*

What things have I struggled with in my life? What lessons did I have to learn again and again? What are the issues in my life that keep circling around me, demanding my attention?

*O God, help me to understand and to be hopeful when my child seems to be repeating the same mistakes. Help me to remember that some lessons take a lifetime to learn.*

## *February 28*

I always sigh with relief when the last day of February comes. I tell myself that we've made it through the worst part of winter. In March, the snows will probably melt away quickly, and soon there will be signs of spring.

Have we made it through the worst part of her teenage years? We seem to have settled into a peaceful coexistence; the rages that left us reeling for many months seem far behind.

Yet, transitions are not always smooth, and they generally don't follow a straight, upward line. We need to try to stay in the peaceful present, but also keep in mind that there may be some difficult changes still to come.

*Holy Lord, let our family rest here in this peaceful place for a while with you, our loving God. We are so very grateful that the worst of the storm seems to be over–for now.*

# March

## *March 1*

I'm sitting alone in the house. All of my children have plans this afternoon. It feels like they don't need me anymore, and this frightens me. I find myself eating everything in sight. I know I'm eating out of loneliness and boredom, trying to fill the hole within me.

As my children begin to move toward others, leaving more space in my life, how do I fill that void? I need to guard against the destructive patterns of mindless activity: drinking too much, over-spending, or overeating.

*Jesus, you went on a journey all alone through the desert, longing for your Heavenly Father to show you the way. Please help me to be quiet when I am alone, to pray for your guidance in order to find out where you wish to lead me next.*

It just burns my brother up that he's working so hard, month after month, and his kids think it's okay not to give anything back. He's so resentful of their laziness, their expectations, and all of their freedom! Yesterday he was despondent and he cried: "When is somebody going to take care of *me* for a change?"

Children need to be useful contributors in their families. We don't do them any favors if we don't expect them to do chores or express gratitude. We end up feeling resentful, and they don't feel good about themselves either. We need to ask, encourage, and enforce their useful participation in our family. Weekly allowances, restriction of privileges, and simply not doing for them until they do for us are some ways to get them to be helpful.

*Mary, at the wedding of Cana you said to your Son, "They have no wine," expecting him to help. Show us, Mary, Mother of God, how to foster our teens' helpfulness and good will, especially when we are feeling overwhelmed by all of life's demands.*

## March 3

We played a game of one-on-one basketball this evening. For once, when I asked he didn't respond with a scornful, "I can't play with my *Mom*!" We had such a great time, laughing and competing. My son finally beat me—the first time ever! His body is almost all muscle now, springing upward, leaping toward the basket, twisting and turning in the air with grace and strength.

Even as my body is slowing down with age, his keeps getting stronger. How can I not mourn the loss of my youth, as I watch my son beginning to enter his prime?

*Dearest Lord, from you all good things flow. In celebrating my son's youthfulness, let me rejoice in all the gifts you have given him, as well as your most exquisite gift to me: my almost grown-up son.*

He's been hanging around with a kid whom we don't like. After they spend time together, our son seems surlier, less respectful. We have tried to tell him our concerns. Should we stop them from being together? Will this boy lead our son astray?

Adolescents try out many personas on their journey to adulthood. Sometimes they are temporarily attracted to someone who exhibits a part of their personality that they are unable to express themselves. We need to communicate our concerns and do our best to monitor worrisome relationships, but ultimately our teens will need to be able to choose their own friends. We must trust that the values we have taught them will continue to influence their decisions.

*Loving Father, hold me in my worry. Help my teen to turn away from the evils of this world and anyone who would try to lead him down a dangerous path. Please watch over him and guide him when I am not there.*

"Adolescents are temporarily brain-damaged."
*Michael J. Bradley, Ed. D.*

With all the physical changes my teen is going through, it's difficult for her to modulate her moods. A huge upheaval is occurring within her. No wonder she's so off-balance—no wonder she seems downright *crazy* at times.

*O God, help me to remember how difficult it was for me to go through my teenage years. Let me be a steady source of strength for my daughter, and help me to trust that I can lean on you when things get too crazy!*

My best friend is going through a divorce. I want to be there for her, but I feel like she's leaning on me too heavily. The relationship has become one-sided. I'm spending more time talking to her than to my own children! My husband tells me to step back from the situation, but I'm so caught up in a whirlwind of confusion.

Sometimes we need to set boundaries around how much we can give to friends. They understand when we become overwhelmed, and usually don't want to become our burden. Sometimes nudging a friend toward prayer, counseling, or ministry to others can help them even more than our continued listening.

*Holy Spirit, help me to gracefully explain to others that I need time apart when I'm feeling depleted. Help them, too, to seek nourishment and support in other places. Fill me with the grace of your love so that I can again be present to my friends when I am replenished.*

Ever since the divorce, my nieces have lived with my brother's ex-wife. When they were younger, he saw them frequently, but now they want to cut back on visitation—again. His daughters say they want to spend more time with their friends, and they can't do that when they go to his house. He knows that there are so few years left of their childhood. Why are they pulling away from him *now*? He feels so helpless.

Visitation needs can be especially challenging when children hit adolescence. We need compassion, creativity, and flexibility to help our teens negotiate between two sets of families, and their authentic need to spend more time with friends.

*Help my brother, Lord, to approach this complex change with an open heart and a mature love. With your help, his family can work together to find a compromise.*

"You're not my *real* mother. I don't have to listen to what you say!"

How these words pierce and wound my best friend. She has been married to her husband for almost five years now, but sometimes she still feels like a newcomer to her family. Will she ever be truly accepted? What more does she need to do to prove her love?

It's not easy being a stepparent. Many times loyalty issues conflict with a teenager's desire to bond. It may help to say, "That's true, I'm not your mother. Tell me about how difficult this must be for you at times." We must be confident about the role we play in our stepchildren's lives, expecting kindness and respect as we give it to them.

*Forgiving God, show us how to reassure our stepchildren of our desire to be a strong, supporting presence in their lives, someone who will cherish them, and, with your help, guide them gracefully into adulthood.*

This evening I brought some supper over to an elderly neighbor whose wife had recently died. When I was late coming through the door, my son asked me (somewhat haughtily) where I had been. "You don't like it when *I'm* not home on time!" he scolded.

Rather than responding with a comment about his lack of compassion, I asked how he felt when I didn't arrive home when expected. He told me he was worried, and wondered what had happened to me. We talked about our neighbor then, and he seemed genuinely concerned. He even offered to shovel his walk the next time it snows.

*Mary, remember how upset and worried you were when you couldn't find Jesus? And how relieved you were when you found him preaching in the Temple? Remind me, Mary, to inform my children of my plans, as I expect them to inform me, and to continually teach them by my actions about the importance of giving to others.*

My neighbor says she sometimes finds herself complaining to her teen about her ex-husband; she can't seem to help herself. She's having such terrible problems communicating right now, and she feels her daughter is the only one who understands. But putting children in the middle—no matter how old they are—is harmful, and can adversely affect their relationship with *both* parents.

No matter how difficult it may be sometimes, we need to restrain our negative feelings about another parent when we are with our children. If we really need to vent, we need to do so with a trusted friend or professional who can counsel us on ways to manage conflicting emotions.

*O Jesus, our Lord and Healer, hear the cry of those who are suffering from a painful divorce. Please heal their suffering and anger. It is especially at these difficult moments that they need to feel your nearness.*

Last night, when I was complaining to my husband about something thoughtless that our son had done, he made a joke that helped put it all in perspective. We laughed, and I felt my anger melting away. It made me realize again how lucky I am to have the gift of such a wonderful spouse to share in this journey of parenting.

How often do I notice all the ways my spouse supports and nourishes me? When do I tell him so? Do I know someone who is struggling though parenthood alone? When did I last do something to help? A phone call, note, or invitation can mean so much to someone who feels isolated and alone.

*Thank you, refreshing God, for all that you have given me. You, who gave the ultimate gift to the world, your Son, Jesus Christ, help me to give the gift of encouragement and love to all whom I encounter.*

My daughter wanted to wear a shirt that was "too tight" to her middle school dance. She told me that "everyone" is wearing them. Reluctantly, I agreed. When I dropped her off at the dance, I couldn't believe what some of the other girls were wearing! My daughter's shirt seemed mild by comparison.

It's hard to balance our children's need to "fit in" with our version of what is appropriate. We must talk with them about projecting an image that doesn't convey the value of their true selves. Yet, society is so over-charged with sexual images, it can sometimes feel like an up-hill battle.

*Holy Spirit, guide my daughter to match her outer self with her "inner" core values. Help me talk with other parents, too, about our shared values and concerns. Together, with your help, we can challenge what society deems "appropriate." We can support each other, and, at the same time, give our daughters back their innocence, bringing them always and ever closer to you.*

"Laughter helps cement those critical bonds of shared fear known only to soldiers in foxholes, cops in squad cars, and parents of troubled adolescents."
*Michael J. Bradley, Ed. D.*

Are there times when I'm taking myself (and my teenager) much too seriously? When is it important to make a joke to ease the tension? It can help to ask the important question: how will this situation look to us ten years from now?

*Sweet and loving God, send us your smiling benevolence. Help us to laugh together more often.*

Tonight when he was coming home late—for about the tenth time—he sailed through the door as if daring us to say a word. We glanced up at him, remembering what our counselor had said, trying to appear nonchalant.

"Aren't you going to yell at me like you usually do? Weren't you even worried?" he asked.

We calmly told him that he knew the consequences, and we refused to get into another confrontation. Later, he genuinely apologized, taking responsibility for his lateness for the very first time.

How are my reactions reinforcing some undesirable behavior in my teen? It takes courage to try something different, but sometimes it's the only way out of a rut we've created for ourselves.

*God, please give me the courage to make the changes so necessary in my relationship with my teen, to move our family toward hope and healing.*

I was outside turning over the flowerbeds, working in the manure and fertilizer, readying them for spring. My son got off the school bus and *without having to be asked*, he grabbed a shovel and started digging. I almost fell over!

When did this new and generous self arrive? Did I miss the signs that it was coming? God wants us to notice his transformative miracles, whenever and wherever they occur.

*Ever-giving God, remind me to be ever mindful of my teen, who is in the process of transforming into a mature and giving young adult, right in front of me!*

My son announces that he's given up vegetables for Lent, and cleaning his room, and, oh yes, studying for exams. We laughed—but then talked about putting more meaning behind his abstentions. We discussed why the season of Lent is so important, sort of like a "spring cleaning" for the soul.

How do I practice my faith on a daily basis? Do I observe holy days arbitrarily? Do I take time to reflect with my teen on the meaning of our spiritual traditions?

*O God, help me to consistently incorporate our faith traditions into family life in ways that take into consideration my teen's particular stage of development and understanding.*

Until he was sixteen, Saint Patrick considered himself a pagan. At that time, he was sold into slavery, and, during his captivity, he became closer to God. He traveled throughout Ireland, converting hundreds of pagans to Christianity. He spent thirty years building schools, churches, and monasteries all over his country.

How much do I know about the saints? What parts of my faith have been redefined by popular folklore or the media rather than truth? When was the last time I read a book about spirituality or religion? When did our family last talk about our faith together?

*Dear Lord, help our family continually to learn about the beauty and wonders of our faith.*

He's begun to shout at us, to tell us to "shut up," sometimes even cursing at us under his breath. We feel like we're bearing the brunt in some unnamed battle. When we react to his behavior, it only seems to get worse; but to ignore it (as some parenting books suggest) conflicts with everything we want to teach him.

Teens often project onto others what they are feeling inside. Could something be happening in school, with his peer group, or his neighborhood friends? What else might make him feel scared, angry, or vulnerable? Instead of retaliating with our own anger at his behavior, we need to guide him toward a better expression of feelings, helping him find other tools for negotiating relationships in and outside our home.

*Be with us, merciful God, in this unfamiliar place. Help us draw closer to our teen, especially when he is lashing out, when we naturally would want to pull away. Guide us in the search for the meaning behind his outbursts, and fill his heart with your love.*

"Remember that always lurking beneath the surface with an adolescent, waiting to make trouble, is the pull not to separate from the parent, not to move forward, not to grow up."

*Anthony E. Wolf, Ph.D.*

I've noticed that my teenager sometimes wants me to do things for her that I thought she had long out-grown. Sometimes her demands seem so unreasonable, almost childish. I know she's capable of doing these things for herself. Maybe I need to recognize that these are the times when she still wants to be taken care of like a child, as a sign of her fear of the ever-widening responsibility of coming to adulthood.

*O God, even your Son, Jesus, had doubts in the garden of Gethsemane about his ability to face the future. Please help my daughter, who is struggling with growing up right now. She needs to feel soothed, and* capable, *and always held by your loving arms.*

Springtime energy. You can almost feel it surging up through the ground. Tiny leaf buds pushing outward. A sluggish world shaking itself off, reawakening, getting re-charged. This afternoon, my daughter and her high school friends went outside without their coats, running and leaping like newborn colts through the grass.

What new part of me needs the energy to spring forth? Where can I best place my springtime energy so it is balanced and of service to my family, my friends, my community, and myself?

*Holy God, Creator of all things, help me spend your gift of energy wisely and joyously, with clarity of purpose and loving intention, rather than wasting my time on foolish pursuits.*

I've noticed her gradually growing, creeping up inch by inch. Suddenly, it happened: she's taller than me! What a strange sensation. She hasn't exactly welcomed comments on this phenomenon, embarrassed, I guess, by all the changes. But this morning she stood up straight (right next to me) and said, "Mom, look who's taller now!"

Secure and feeling good in her own skin. What a blessing! Not always do our teens feel so pleased with their growing bodies.

*Mary, our Mother, you took such loving care of our Lord, your Son, Jesus. You watched him grow from a little boy into a man. Please help my daughter continue to accept and nourish her body, embracing each stage of the maturing process.*

My father died last week. What a sad time! Although he had been very ill for a while, none of us expected it. The grief is overwhelming; it has brought up so many feelings and memories. I've been so busy helping my mother and siblings get through it, I'm not sure how my teenagers are coping.

*Merciful God, allow me the time to grieve this loss. Please hold my children in their grief, too. Help us respect the different ways that we grieve, and support each other during this difficult time.*

My daughter has been quiet lately, not as exuberant since her grandfather died. Could this be affecting her more than she will admit? She didn't seem at all upset at the funeral; I noticed that she didn't even cry.

"Is there really a heaven? What happens to our bodies when we die? Will you die too, and leave me someday?" The death of a loved one generates so many questions for our children and teens.

Teenagers are still children, and children grieve differently than adults. After losing a grandparent or another significant person in their lives, children initially may not want to add to our burden, and some can try to hide their feelings. It's normal for them to take more time to process a loss, or to experience a delayed reaction months later. The reality of death can bring them to a keener awareness of the vulnerability of life. While difficult, it can be a rich time of life, bringing them closer and more deeply to God.

*Loving Father, give me the courage to talk to my teens about the deeper issues of pain and loss, which bring both of us sadness and tears. Watch over her during this sad and questioning time.*

"When we surrender, we open ourselves up to the mystery of life, to the risks of the future, to the challenge of the unknown."

*Joyce Rupp*

When have I last given up control over something? What do I need to surrender? Sometimes when our children are making the huge, but gradual transition into becoming adolescents, we want to hold tightly to the "old" way of doing things—but this can get us stuck. How will I know when it is time to plunge forward, with a leap of faith, into my new and changing role as the parent of a new and growing teenager? I guess I won't know, but it *will* happen—whether I want it to or not!

*God of mystery, surround me with your infinite wisdom as I begin the journey of parenting a young teen. I yearn to feel your risen presence in me as I put my trust in your capable hands.*

Last night, I nervously shared with a friend a huge problem I had been having with my daughter. She told me that she had experienced almost the very same thing when her kids were teenagers! I felt such relief. I had been feeling so alone, so ashamed and unsure. When she told me how she dealt with this problem, and how it eventually passed, it gave me hope and a new perspective. In our tear-filled eyes, we found a moment of grace.

*I praise you, O God, for coming to me through the eyes and words of a dear friend. Help me to notice your presence in everyone I meet. Help me to hear your comforting words spoken by those who love me. Give me the courage to share my pain, and to receive your grace through another's counsel.*

## *March 26*

Every time I talk with this one particular parent, I walk away feeling so deflated. She brags about all her daughter's activities, her perfect grades, and how she's going to have her pick of *the very best* colleges. It makes me anxious and worried that my daughter isn't doing enough, that I'm somehow not good enough.

When others feel the need to *constantly* inflate themselves (or their children), it usually comes from an inability to connect in a more honest and humble way. Often they don't even realize how they come across to others. If her words are uncovering an anxiety deep within me, can I hand that worry over to God?

*Dear God, help me to set my insecure heart aside and to value my daughter for her unique gifts and strengths. Help me to trust that through you, she is becoming all she is meant to be.*

My brother's daughter says she can't handle the custody battle between him and her mother. Things have turned spiteful and mean. They accuse each other of terrible things and can't even have a civil conversation. His daughter says that after she leaves for college, she's never coming back. She's looking forward to leaving them already, and she's only thirteen!

Children suffer terribly when their parents are involved in a messy divorce. We must look to our adult selves and work through our angry feelings. But this can be so difficult! Sometimes it seems impossible. If we can't manage it alone, we need to get assistance from a more neutral party, so our children will not continue being wounded by the two people whom they love the most.

*Jesus, my Christ, please guide my brother and his wife toward a place of forgiveness and compassion. You have healed so many. For the sake of this child, help them to overcome their anger and to reach toward solutions, which will involve compromise and healing.*

"I'm sorry. I was wrong."

These words, when spoken with true intention can be incredibly healing. So why do I resist saying them? Does it diminish my effectiveness with my teen to admit that I've made a mistake?

The opposite is true. When we have the courage to make amends for our wrongdoing, we show our children that *everyone* makes mistakes. When we don't offer rationalizations for our bad behavior, our apologies can be heard by our teen as genuine and sincere—and the appropriate way to behave when we do something wrong.

*Forgiving Father, allow me to recognize the times when a sincere apology is needed. Help me not to let my foolish pride get in the way of taking responsibility for my transgressions.*

"I hate you! I'll never forgive you!"

"But...you don't understand...I was only trying to..."

Unfortunately, we have the capacity to inflict the most pain on those whom we hold most dear. When we try to rationalize or explain away our actions, we aren't truly listening to our child's pain. Instead, we are making excuses for our behavior, the very thing that we ask them *not* to do.

It takes a mature spirit to listen without defensiveness to how we have wounded another.

*God of all healing, help me to say the words, "Tell me more about how I have hurt you. I want to understand, completely, the depth of your pain."*

Last night we had a spring snowstorm. We were almost knee-deep in snow. Then it warmed up to sixty-five degrees this afternoon and the sun melted it all away. We didn't even have to shovel!

We don't always have to *do* something when our teens are storming around the house. Sometimes they just need to bluster and blow. Not paying any attention is sometimes the best course—as long as they're not doing it all the time! Often, our teens can work out their problem on their own, and, moments later, they've completely forgotten it existed.

*God, give me shelter when the springtime storms of adolescence start to blow. Let me feel comforted by the knowledge that they rarely last too long, that they don't cause much damage–if we know when to stay out of their way!*

**Not over-reacting** 

"March comes in like a lion and goes out like a lamb."

Adolescence is like this, too. Some teens will roar when they begin to assert their need for independence. Eventually, the roars become less frequent and less intense. The lamb will reappear, surprising us with gentleness and an extraordinary capacity to return our love.

*Help me, Lamb of God, to welcome the "lamb" in my teen.*

# April

"Oh to be only half as wonderful as my child thought I was when he was small, and only half as stupid as my teenager now thinks I am."

*Rebecca Richards*

How do I handle my teen's comments about my ineptitude? Do those comments make me angry? Do I believe them? Does it make me engage in foolish self-doubt or recrimination?

All teens go through a stage when they think their parents don't know anything; when they think that they do know it all. It's only their way of compensating for a persistent fear over *not* knowing it all. It's their way of separating and moving away from childhood.

*O Mary, did you struggle when Jesus first began to show signs of his independence? Still, you also put your trust and faith in the will of God. Help me, Mary, to feel your love as my teen begins to assert himself. Help me to put my faith in the desire of God to see us through.*

Everything is fresh and green and bursting with life, except my daughter. She sits in her room for hours. She doesn't want to go to school. She doesn't seem to want to do anything. She's neglecting her friends. She's tired all the time. Something isn't right. Is she sick or could she be depressed?

Undiagnosed depression is dangerous and can sometimes lead to worsening mental illness or suicide. Asking our teens if they feel like hurting themselves will not plant that idea in their heads; on the contrary, it may help them to talk about a very lonely and scary feeling before acting on it. We need to ask the hard questions and seek immediate help from a professional if we have *any* doubts about a teen's mental health.

*O God, I am so worried. Please watch over my daughter. Help us through this dark and scary time.*

Sometimes when I'm driving my son to (or from) his activities, I'm tempted to call a friend. Surprisingly, if I leave the cell phone alone, I find it's during these drives that we seem to catch up on things. He willingly tells me about his day, and I feel more connected when we finally get home.

We need to remember that for most teens it's easier to open up when we're engaged in another activity, like driving, shopping, or watching a sporting event—when they feel we're not going to pounce on their every word.

*Help me, O God, to maximize these windows of opportunity to connect with my teen. Remind me that countless little moments will lead up to a lifetime of love.*

A friend called recently to ask a time-consuming, but frivolous favor. I said yes even though I had a hundred other things to do that day. Saturdays are my catch-up day; still, I did the favor. Then I spent the rest of the afternoon feeling resentful, shuttling my teenager to all of her activities. At the end of the day, I was exhausted, and my husband was annoyed that I was too tired for "us." And then the next day I slept in and neglected to go to church.

How often do I find myself saying yes, when I really should be saying no?

The Lord asks us to love our neighbor "as" ourselves—not more or less than ourselves. We need to prioritize the tasks that deserve our attention, and not deplete our energies unreasonably. In this busy time of our lives, when we have more than enough to do, we must discern which activities will bring us closer to God.

*Help me, loving God, to say "no" to frivolous things, so that I may have the energy to say "yes" to the wonder of you.*

His grades this quarter are a whole grade lower in every subject, and he doesn't seem to care. He's been nasty and irritable for weeks at a time. Our son seems an entirely different person, lashing out at us without provocation. He picks at his food, telling us he isn't hungry. I don't understand what's wrong. Nothing I say or do seems to help.

Teenage depression has many faces. When irritability becomes the norm, when grades drop, or when there is a change in eating or sleeping patterns for over two weeks, it's time to get professional help—fast.

*Merciful God, please help my son. He seems so far away and out of reach. Guide me toward the best possible care for my teen. I trust that you will show us the way toward health and healing.*

"Our health is best served by participating in those activities that are in our own highest and best interests. This is not selfish. It is the very basis for a healthy life. There is not a single cell in our bodies that flourishes through sacrificing its own health for the health of the surrounding cells."

*Christiane Northrup, M.D.*

When am I putting my own needs on hold for the sake of extra activities? When am I denying myself spiritual nourishment out of a lack of time? Where am I *constantly* sacrificing my need for God for the sake of another?

All we need to do sometimes is say, "Oh, thank you so much for considering me. But I really must say no this time." Complicated explanations aren't necessary.

*Dear God, please show me how to say no sometimes to the demands that others would put on my time. Unless I truly have the time and energy, and am able to say yes* willingly, *help me to say no* gracefully.

"Parents often think their kid is just being a kid, that all teens are moody, oppositional, and irritable all the time...but the typical teenager should be more like "Happy Days" than "Rebel without a Cause."

*Madelyne Gould*

Reckless behavior, extreme sensitivity to rejection or failure, and loss of interest in friends may signal the onset of teenage depression. It can be dangerous to write off a teen's worsening symptoms as a normal part of adolescence.

*Jesus, please help me to notice and recognize the signs of depression if they appear in my teen. Help us during the dark and lonely times. Show me the way, O Lord, for I am afraid.*

The doctor thinks my daughter needs to be medicated for her depression. What if the medication is addictive? What if she experiences terrible side effects? I once read about a teenager on anti-depressants who killed his whole family!

It's frightening to think that our child may need medication to help her cope with the disease of depression. We sometimes blame ourselves for the illness, and become more anxious because we haven't seen all the signs. Most antidepressants today are safe, but physicians do not recommend medication lightly. If indicated, most doctors now see the benefits of taking medication as far outweighing the risks.

*God, help me to trust the professionals who are treating my teen. Give me the strength to gather all the necessary information that we will need during this important time.*

Today is my son's birthday. How is it that he is a teenager already? Wasn't it just yesterday that I carried him, squirming and kicking in my womb? I remember when it was time for him to be born, how he raced down the birth canal, so anxious to be in the world.

*God of life, open my eyes to see this teenager being birthed in front of me. Let me be alert and aware as he makes his way into this new and sometimes dangerous world. Remind me that inside him are many selves: the baby, the little boy, and the man he will someday, too soon, become. Thank you, gracious God, for the gift of my wonderful son.*

After nearly a week of rain, the tulip bulbs I planted last fall have finally come up—in the most glorious shade of red! I remember the day I planted them; it was dark and dreary, and I was worried about how my daughter was adjusting to her new school. She hadn't made any friends yet, and was coming home each day so sad and lonely. I planted every bulb with a silent prayer that my daughter could handle this transition; that everything would eventually work out.

She is so happy now! With wonderfully spirited friends, she's involved in school activities and doing well with her teachers and classes. She even has a springtime smile!

*Sometimes hope is small, like the size of a tulip bulb in the palm of our hand. Then God comes along to make hope bloom. Thank you, O God, you who hold the blossom of my heart.*

Our daughter's new best friend is in trouble. She told our daughter, in an almost bragging way, how she's cut herself on her arm. She hides it by wearing long sleeves, so her parents won't find out. We don't want to interfere because our daughter fears the repercussions. We fear them, too. What if her parents stop talking to us, or become defensive? Or worse yet, do nothing to help their daughter?

When children cut themselves it's an expression of a deeper pain; they cut to make their pain more visible and tangible. Would I want someone to tell me if they knew my child was in trouble? The answer is, *yes*, of course. We have a responsibility to do everything in our power as Christians to help a child in need.

*Lord God, give me the courage to tell the truth to those who may need to hear it. Help me to hear the truth from others who have the courage to share it with me. Let my friends and neighbors receive my compassion and desire to help with openness and trust.*

Last week, when I was in the school office, I saw my son's friend waiting to see the principal. The boy looked upset, and said he was in trouble for something he'd done in class. I hesitated about offering advice, but then, on a whim, I said, "Well, just take responsibility for your part in it, and things will come out okay." Later, his mother told me how her son had related the whole incident to her when he came home. She said he heard what I had said, and that he felt so good about himself for admitting what he had done.

Sometimes I am fearful to get involved, and I wonder how others will perceive my words.

*God, help me to remember that if my intentions are pure, your words will flow from me to help those who need to hear them, for I am your servant.*

**Risking the right words**

## *April 13*

One day my seventeen-year-old wants to be a nurse, the next day a lawyer, then a hairdresser or a model. She's so unfocused and unclear. I'm not sure how to deal with all this indecision. Shouldn't she have a more specific goal by now?

Am I always *completely* sure of my direction? Have I become the person I set out to be? One of the major tasks of adolescence is to explore identity. In order for that to happen, there will be many twists and turns along the way.

*Help her, O God, as her process of "becoming" unfolds. Show her that the freedom to continually explore herself and her goals will never end. Help me to trust that through your eternal love she will become the person she is meant to be.*

We are waiting to hear from colleges. Most of the other kids in his class have gotten their acceptance letters, some from very prestigious universities. Every day he rushes to check the mail. So much expectation! His grades weren't the greatest. What if he isn't accepted into a "good" school?

There are many wonderful colleges and places of learning in the world. Attending the "best" college doesn't necessarily determine future success in life—although modern society seems to think it does. We need to encourage our teens to find a school or vocation that is the best fit for them, and to not feel "less than" if it's not a "big name" school, or one that "everybody" else is attending.

*God of anticipation, watch over my child. Remind him that sometimes things don't work out* our *way, but they always work out* your *way.*

When my neighbor gets home from work, he always has at least one beer. Then he has one or two glasses of wine with dinner. Relaxing in front of the TV, he usually has several more drinks. He tells his wife that this is his way of taking care of himself. She tells me all of this tearfully, over coffee. She's concerned. She thinks he drinks too much, but he says he's not out in bars. He can't see how this is hurting her and the kids. He thinks he can control it. He holds down a good job. Does she have a right to be upset?

One rule of thumb: when someone in our family has a problem with our drinking, then our drinking has become a problem. Alcoholism is a progressive disease, rooted in secrecy and shame. A big part of alcohol abuse is denial, and the first step is having the courage to recognize that there is a problem.

*O God, help this woman find the courage to seek assistance (from self-help groups like A.A. or her pastor or a therapist) to deal with this problem so she and her family will always feel safe and loved. Please give this man the courage to hear why his drinking has become a problem for someone he loves and the strength to work toward a healthier lifestyle.*

Last week, our neighbor's son asked about getting a keg of beer for the party he's planning at their house after the prom. He's eighteen and drinks, and so do most of his friends. She's not sure what to tell him. The legal drinking age is twenty-one, but she rationalizes that it would be better to have the kids at her home, drinking under her supervision—with her holding all the car keys—than having them driving around and getting killed!

To make it easier for teens to gain access to illegal substances of *any* kind—*even* alcohol, even under supervision—is *wrong*. Alcohol poisoning, the choice to have sex, and the progression to other drugs, are only a few of the disastrous consequences of supplying alcohol to teens.

*Help us, God, to find other parents who can support us on this important issue. Help us to monitor our own drinking behaviors as our teens notice not only what we say, but what we* do.

On Friday, I packed for a weekend visit with an old friend. We were going to spend the whole weekend together: hiking, shopping, and catching up on each other's lives. Still, as I prepared to leave I wondered if it would be worth it? Would my family be able to manage the whole weekend without me?

...It was *wonderful* to spend time with my friend. When I returned, I felt recharged and refreshed and ready to step back into my busy life. Except for a few mishaps, everyone managed just fine without me, and, in fact, they seemed truly glad to see me and were more appreciative of all the little things I do.

We all need freedom from responsibility now and then. Our families seem to appreciate us more when we take the time to replenish ourselves.

*Loving God, from whom all good things flow, remind me how important it is to nourish myself, both with and apart from my growing family.*

I had always felt secure in the fact that my fourteen-year-old daughter hadn't smoked, drank, or experimented with drugs. I had been very involved in her life, vigilant about knowing who her friends were and where she spent most of her time. Imagine my shock when she came up to me one day and said "Mom, I tried pot." After I picked myself up off the floor, I asked: Where? How? When? She told me that once, when we were visiting friends, their daughter had been smoking and offered her some, and so she tried it.

On the bright side, my daughter told me that she didn't like smoking it, would never do it again, and actually felt sorry for the girl who offered it!

No matter how hard we try to protect our teens, they will be constantly navigating a world that can be dangerous, and presented with many chances for making tough decisions.

*Thank you, God, for giving my daughter the trust to talk to me about such a significant issue without fearing my judgment or rage. Please continue to watch over her and help her to make safer and wiser decisions in the future.*

## *April 19*

Last night we held a monthly meeting of a group of parents who want to help prevent substance abuse among the youth in our town—it's a big problem! As usual, only a handful of people showed up. One of our group members complained that the parents who *should* be there never are. "All of us here already know what needs to be done," she said. It can be so discouraging sometimes.

Families lead incredibly busy lives. It's important to keep in mind that just because only a handful of people show up for a meeting, it doesn't mean that no one else in the community cares.

*O Jesus, you know what it's like to feel all alone, trying to teach people why it's important to love and care for one another. Help us find ways to communicate and reach out to other parents in the community, knowing that even a small gesture can create a ripple of change.*

"He can push my buttons like nobody else. Sometimes I just hate my own kid!"

A colleague confided this to me at the office coffeepot. I told him I've felt exactly the same way. Then we laughed at the absurdity of raising teenagers. After complaining, we talked about how we don't really *hate* them, but sometimes it's hard not to *intensely dislike* the things they do.

It can be frightening and difficult to come to grips with the powerful feelings our teenagers can evoke in us. It feels good to vent them with someone who understands. Sharing with others normalizes the situation and gives us enough sustenance for days or even weeks at a time. It seems we have more room to notice all the wonderful things about our teen, once we've vented our anger.

*Help me, Holy Spirit, to take the risk of sharing my thoughts and feelings with others. It will make me (and the person with whom I'm sharing) stronger and wiser for the days ahead.*

I'm off to another committee meeting tonight. I volunteered to be on this committee, but it's taking up a lot of my time. Lately, I've been leaving the kids alone too often on weeknights. They are certainly old enough to be alone, but I don't like it. Before leaving, I shared this feeling with my daughter, and she said, "We can handle it. Besides, think of all the good things you're doing."

I paused before going out the door because it seemed like she was hesitating. "But, Mom?" she added, smiling. "Just don't sign up for anything else."

When our children see us sacrificing our personal time for the good of others, it shows them the importance of giving. But if they see us continually sacrificing, without paying attention to their needs, we are teaching them that we value *others* more than we value *them*.

*Gracious God, show me how to find a prayerful balance in my life. Help me continue to teach the importance of giving by example, but to remember it is my responsibility to give to my family* first.

Our son was caught smoking in the school bathroom—again. He got a detention, but the school suggested that we may want to do more. We know smoking is bad for him, but both of us smoke, so how can we tell *him* to stop?

Smoking can be an extremely dangerous "gateway" to substance abuse for teens, possibly leading to other drugs and a lifetime of nicotine addiction; it's also closely linked to teenage depression. We can use this experience as an opportunity to offer help to our teen to stop smoking. We can also examine our own smoking behaviors and explore ways in which we might begin to lead healthier lives together.

*O God, hear our prayer. Addictions are powerful. I'm afraid this addiction has us firmly in its unhealthy grasp. Lift us up from the place where we would choose "it" over you, the Lord who created us and who loves us. You desire us to be free of our addictions, to be healthy and strong.*

Last night we had another family over for dinner. Our daughter didn't run off to play with the other children, but sat with us at the table for a long time, listening and contributing to the conversation. We were so proud of her ability to communicate her own ideas maturely with the adults who were present.

By observing adults, my teen can experiment with the "adult" part of herself that is beginning to emerge. How often do I entertain friends in my home to give my teen this opportunity?

*Jesus, remind me to invite my neighbors and friends into my home, in the spirit of your holy name, so we all may benefit from the company and conversation.*

I smelled alcohol as soon as my son and his friends got into the car. They were laughing—too loudly, too boisterously! I panicked. All I could think of was getting them home. When we got back to our house, I blasted my son and told him he was grounded for the rest of his life! The next morning, we talked about what happened rationally. Strangely, it was as if there were no barriers between us. My son poured his heart out, telling me things I hadn't noticed or known about before.

If our teens make mistakes when they are still living at home, we can use that experience to help them be more prepared to navigate other dangers when they're out on their own, by asking them what they may have learned from the experience, and assuring that they receive appropriate consequences. We need to have continuing conversations about the hard and scary issues. Our teens need to know where we stand on these important issues, and learn what our faith would tell us is the right thing to do.

*God, my Father, you who love me in all of my imperfections, show me how to see my teen's mistakes as opportunities, as signals for lessons that still need learning; for discussion; for growth, as he matures into a whole human being, never perfect, but always my child, and always your beloved.*

"Yet how are we to help them become separate, independent persons? By allowing them to do things for themselves, by permitting them to wrestle with their own problems, by letting them learn from their own mistakes."

*Adele Farber*

When was the last time I allowed my teenager to think through a decision on her own? When did I not jump in with advice or opinions?

*God of infinite wisdom, show me that I don't always know what's best for my teen. And even if I do, isn't it so much better when she can figure it out for herself?!*

"Can I go? Why can't I? Why won't you let me? All the other kids are going. I've got to! You don't understand how important this is. I'll never get this chance again. Tell me your answer! I have to know RIGHT NOW."

We don't have to make decisions quickly, although the pressure to make them during those "teenage moments" can feel enormous. It's especially when we're feeling pressured that we need to step back and ask the important questions: Will there be supervision? What will you say if someone offers you drugs or alcohol? Who else is planning to go? Can you give me the phone numbers for some of the other parents?

*God, give me the presence of mind to ask all the questions I need to ask, without feeling pressured into making a hasty decision. If I'm still feeling wary when I have all the facts, give me the courage to say "no."*

"Mom!! She did it again... Dad!!! She just ruined my favorite shirt."

"No, I didn't. She's lying. And besides, she took my CD!"

Our children have the opportunity to learn the valuable skills of negotiation and compromise if we allow and *expect* them to resolve disputes without our interference. There are times, however, when intervention is required, including cases of physical violence or other forms of abuse, or when they just can't figure out how to do it without our help.

We need to give each of them a chance to present their side of the story to the other without interruption, saying "This is what bothered me. This is what I need from you. This is what I'm willing to do differently next time." If the other child can rephrase what he's heard before presenting his side of the story, the first child will feel truly listened to—then they can switch places, allowing for a healing dialogue between them.

*Dear God, help me to be an effective model of how to resolve differences with others by listening to my teens and teaching them respect and the willingness to compromise.*

This afternoon, I congratulated a friend on her teen's academic achievements. Her daughter's name appeared in our school bulletin for winning an important award. She said, "She's a smart cookie, my Jennifer, not that I can take any credit for it." I replied, "Well, you certainly had something to do with it." She added, "Yes, but I learned long ago that they really are their own selves."

On the good days, we would love to take credit for our children's accomplishments. On the bad days, it's easy to want to place the blame somewhere (anywhere!) else. It's important to remember that our children *really are their own selves* and they have the ability to make choices in moving or *not* moving toward their goals.

*Gentle Father, help me to recognize that my teen's accomplishments are as much a reflection of her* ability *to do well at something, as my success at parenting. Help me to love and support my child, O God, no matter what her accomplishments, just as you always love me.*

**They really are their own selves** 

"The clever see the danger and hide;
But the simple go on, and suffer for it."

*Proverbs 27:12*

Timing is everything with an adolescent. Do I tend to approach him about a serious subject when he's tired or cranky? Do I demand that he do a chore when he's in the middle of homework or watching his favorite television show? I shouldn't be surprised if my teenager isn't receptive when I ask things of him at the right time for me, but the wrong time for *him*.

Certain chores and tasks need to be done immediately, but asking "when?" for the things that can wait models the importance of respecting his growing ability and desire to manage his own time.

*Help me God, to be considerate of his time and space, as I want him to be considerate in helping with chores around the house.*

Today we went to one of my daughter's softball games. To be honest, a part of me didn't want to go—many of the parents don't go to the games anymore, and she didn't seem that interested in whether or not I was planning to attend. I'd had such a busy week, and so many chores were begging to be done. Still, I went and sat for two hours on a cool bleacher, in the misty rain wondering if it made any difference to her that I was there.

They lost the game, miserably, but immediately after the game, she ran up to me and asked, "Did you see it? Did you see it? Did you see my play?" And I was so glad I was there to answer with a resounding, "Yes!"

What she really meant was, "Did you see *me*?"

When we returned home, the chores were still there. The chores will *always* be there, but someday my teenager will not.

*Thank you, all-seeing God, for helping me to recognize the importance of* really *seeing my child.*

# May

Lately I have found myself getting tense with my son. I'm constantly "on" him to do *better*, to try *harder*; to achieve *more*, and it's causing a strain between us. I know it's irrational; he's a good kid. I know he's doing the best he can. But I remember how I got into trouble when I was his age, my parents divorced, and I lost a beloved grandparent—all at age sixteen. I have some ideas about where all of my unrealistic expectations are coming from, yet I can't seem to change my behavior.

Sometimes irrational behavior comes from our response to unresolved issues from our childhood. Hidden memories of divorce, death, or other traumatic events can often trigger anxiety. If the magnitude of a response to a situation puzzles us, it can help to examine what happened in our lives when we were the age that our children are *now*. Sometimes just having this awareness can break us out of a potentially destructive pattern.

*Help me, O God, to delve into my past when necessary in order to understand the present. Bring the knowledge of my "teenage self" into this relationship with my teen, and guide me toward wisdom, acceptance, and compassion.*

"The best substitute for experience is being sixteen."
*Raymond Duncan*

Did we once think we knew the answers to everything? Did we engage in risky behaviors that are hard to face up to now? If we did some things during our teenage years that we are ashamed of, it may be difficult to gain a healthy perspective when we see similar behaviors emerging in our own teenagers. Or we may become overly focused on what they *could* be doing wrong, rather than focusing on what they *are* doing right. Our teens aren't destined to repeat our wrongdoings, nor do they need to know every detail of our past. What is helpful is an approach that incorporates self-revelation when appropriate, and expectations that are clear and morally strong for what we believe in *today*.

*O God, please forgive me for the mistakes of my past. Show me with the grace of your love, how to guide my child toward a life that is honest and productive, decent, loving, and happy.*

Glory be to him whose power, working in us, can do infinitely more than we can ask or imagine.

*Cf. Ephesians 3:20*

Our best friend's wife has been diagnosed with cancer! We are so frightened for them, and there's so much that needs to be done: at his job, at the house, taking his wife to doctor appointments. He's been relying on his eldest daughter to pick up some of the slack, but sometimes we wonder if it's too much for her.

When we are in the middle of an adult-focused crisis, it can be hard to pay attention to our children's needs. We hope our teens can hold on, and help out for a while, as we struggle to cope with an enormous burden. It can be easy to forget that we don't necessarily have to lean so heavily on our teens, nor do we need to do it all ourselves. We can turn to neighbors and friends or people in our church community, who would be willing to lend a hand, if we would only ask.

*Holy God, release this family from their fear and pride. Help us to convince them to let us inform others about the extent of their family's pain, so that through you we may be able to offer them the help they so desperately need. Please watch over their family during this stressful time.*

Sometimes our daughter is so nasty! Everyone tells us how nice, kind, and accomplished she is—a completely different person when she's outside of our home. So what are we doing wrong that makes her treat us this way? It's hard for us not to take it personally.

It's not unusual for our teenagers to "let it all hang out" at home. After all, everyone deserves a "meltdown" once in a while. However, this doesn't mean we have to just sit there and take it if it's happening all the time. We need to help our teens learn how to modulate and deal with their frustrations in more appropriate ways.

If she has the capacity to be nice and respectful toward others, then she can act that way at home, too. Letting her know that her behaviors and attitudes are choices under her control can help, especially if we don't overreact to her meltdowns.

*God, help me be placid in the face of her fury, and give me the strength to hold firm to reasonable limits.*

With the start of longer days, he's out with his friends all the time. All he wants to do is drive—and he does every chance he gets. I miss having him around. Then—surprise! Last night he stayed home and asked if I'd play Ping-Pong with him. I had plans, but I immediately dropped everything. We spent over an hour together, with him gloating—and me groaning over his every win.

At this stage, most teens want to be in charge of managing their time. Instead of complaining that they're never home, it's much more effective to have them figure out that they miss us and want to spend time with us once in awhile.

*Open and loving God, help me be available whenever I sense my teen needs to spend some time with me. Don't let me miss this increasingly rare opportunity to show him my love. Keep me from harboring resentment as he becomes increasingly involved in the world around him.*

He had a car accident last night. Nothing too serious, no one got hurt, thank God, but we were all pretty shaken. He came home in tears, full of remorse and apologies, wanting to make amends.

How grateful we are when the worst doesn't happen, when our children survive unharmed and can learn from their experience. How proud we are when they take responsibility for their mistakes. How worried we are about what *might have been*.

*Blessed God, thank you for watching over my teen as he ventures out into a world filled with danger and uncertainty. Please help him to be more cautious when he's driving. Hold me in my worry, Father. I am frightened and I don't want to let him go.*

Sometimes when I tell my daughter how I feel about something, all she does is shake her head, other times she looks like she isn't even listening. It's so frustrating! I wonder if anything I say is getting through at all.

When I shared this with my mother-in law, she told me that she used to wonder about the same thing. It wasn't until many years later that her own daughter (my sister-in-law) came to her and said, "You know those little things you used to say? And I acted like I didn't care? It helped. It really did make a difference."

A moment of God's grace can come to us from all sorts of unexpected places! We may not envision our older friends, neighbors, and relatives as having experienced the same sort of parenting issues with their children as we do now with our own. But they often have had similar experiences, and they can offer us words of wisdom and a different perspective, if we are open to what they have to say.

*Dear God, show me how to be open and accepting of many different sources of parenting advice, so that I can learn from those who have gone before me, and light the way for those yet to come.*

Yesterday afternoon, instead of nagging my son for about the hundredth time to remove his muddy shoes from the living room, I threw them outside under a bush. Maybe that was extreme, but I guess I was at the end of my rope. It took him about ten minutes to find them this morning. Boy was he mad! But this evening I noticed that he had put his muddy shoes in the garage, where they belong, as soon as he came home from school.

Sometimes we need to stop *talking* and start *doing*.

*Patient God, help me to have reasonable expectations of my children. Guide me to react in appropriate, yet surprising ways if those expectations aren't met sometimes.*

Last night, the police called from the mall near our house. My son and his friend were caught shoplifting from a music store. I was mortified and angry, furious that he would do something like that. I don't even remember how I got myself to the mall. The store manager looked at me as if I were the worst parent in the entire world. But when I saw my son's frightened and tearful expression, my anger faded away. My eyes filled with tears and I hugged him, telling him that I was there for him and that somehow we would work it out.

Our teenagers will make mistakes; sometimes rather big mistakes. It can be difficult not to explode, but by showing them compassion instead of anger, they will usually accept responsibility for their actions instead of blaming us for getting angry and *not* understanding. In this way, these experiences can show our teens and us more about ourselves and help us to avoid the same mistakes later.

*Dear God, help me to remain levelheaded during times of crisis. Remind me to use my teen's mistakes as a vehicle for teaching morals. Through your grace, may these moments be a chance for me to display compassion and a steady, loving presence to my teen.*

"People are often unreasonable, illogical, and self-centered: forgive them anyway."

*Mother Teresa*

Teenagers probably display these traits best of all. During adolescence, teens are trying out their "adult" selves, but they often overestimate what they think they know or can do. They are spending time developing their identity and sorting out their place in the sometimes-scary world around them. Their bodies are changing at a rapid rate with an influx of hormones. They need to bolster their egos in order to take steps toward separation from us; this false bravado and inflated sense of self helps them have the courage to make the next step toward adulthood. Still, the constant mood-swings, and "know it all" attitude is enough to drive most of us crazy!

*Jesus, sometimes it's hard for me to let go of my anger. Lord, you forgive the most despicable of sins; please forgive me when I don't want to forgive. Please help me when my teen is being pig-headed, self-centered, or unreasonable. Help me to "forgive him anyway."*

Yesterday I played my best round of golf ever. It was a gorgeous day, a gentle breeze was blowing, and the shots I made seemed effortless. I was in "the zone." It was so nice to be able to unwind for a few hours with some friends. But later, on my drive home, I felt guilty for not spending that time doing things for or with my family.

It can be difficult to balance personal needs with those of our family. We need to nurture ourselves, but if we find ourselves *regularly* needing an escape route, and *regularly* neglecting the needs of our family, then we need to re-examine our commitments and the ways we spend our leisure time.

*Guide me, O Lord, to take care of myself spiritually, physically, and emotionally, while always striving to stay aware of my family's needs.*

Mother's Day. My children used to jump on my bed, still in their pajamas, with kisses and homemade cards and declarations of love. Oh, how I miss those sweet kisses! What I wouldn't give to have my babies again—if only for a day!

We must remember that our teens love us just as fiercely as they did when they were children, and they still do need us—even if they don't always show it in the ways we might expect.

*O Mary, you know all about the difficulties of being a mother and the pain of having to share our children with the rest of the world. Help me to be open to the surprises my children may still have in store for me, and to welcome all expressions of love that they choose to give.*

"You're so clueless. You have no idea who I really am."

*Anonymous teenager*

What she was *really* saying is: "It's so scary here all alone. I wish I could talk to you about some of the things I am experiencing. I wish you knew some of what I have to go through."

When our teen says something outlandish, it may help to focus on the feelings behind the words. Sometimes agreeing is a wonderful way to begin: "You're right. I don't have a clue. Tell me what it's like being you. I want to understand." Parenting a teen often means learning different ways of communicating.

*God of infinite wisdom, guide me in new ways of talking and relating with my teen.*

My neighbor's son was caught with marijuana at school. The police charged him with possession of drugs. His father's first response was to get a good lawyer to try to get the charges dropped. We're flabbergasted! What kind of message is he sending to his son if this succeeds?

As parents, we want to do everything in our power to protect our children. But when that includes enabling them to bypass the consequences of their actions, we're not doing them any favors. Trying to "beat the system" will only teach this teen that it doesn't matter what he does—as long as he doesn't get caught.

*Merciful God, it can be so hard to allow my teen to suffer the consequences of his behavior. At those times, help me to remember that I am teaching him important life lessons in responsibility.*

**Don't let them off the hook** 

Then Peter came and said to him, "...How should I forgive? As many as seven times?"

Jesus said to him, "Not seven times, but, I tell you, seventy times seven."

*Matthew 18:21*

We need to develop the capacity to forgive our children (and ourselves) over and over again. Many times, we will encounter the same mistakes and offences before we all get it right. It helps to not take the things they do as a personal attack, but rather as a part of their emerging need for independence.

*Allow me, my Christ, to let the light of forgiveness enter my heart,* seventy times seven times, *and even more.*

It seems my son is doing something to make me angry every other minute. It's as if he does it on purpose: not taking out the garbage, tormenting his sister, back talking. Then he says he's sorry—like that's supposed to make everything okay, and I'm supposed to quickly forgive him, just like that. And I usually do. But then he turns around ten minutes later and does the exact same thing! I'm so tired of this! When is he going to get it? When is this all going to end?

I have to remind myself that it will end. In the meantime, I don't have to forgive too quickly if I am to expect a demonstrated behavior change. If I continue to give in when my teens treat me badly, he will get the message that others will tolerate his bad behavior—and this is not a lesson I want to teach him. Teens don't feel very good about themselves when we allow them to act this way.

*O God, help me know when my teen is taking advantage of me. It's hard to find a balance between love and discipline. I need your help in setting clearer boundaries with my teen, knowing that this will ultimately help my teen draw closer to you.*

This afternoon I walked to a field near my house. It was a gorgeous, sunny day, and the big puffs of white clouds seemed close enough to touch, but hid the warmth of the sun. I lay down on a blanket and gazed up at the clouds. I stayed there for at least half an hour. It felt so good to rest for a while; I was filled with awe. It was as if God was there beside me saying, "Yes, rest now, and behold what I have created."

When was the last time I took some time alone to find God? We can become so busy with our "to do" lists that we scurry to get through each day, not paying attention to the world around us. We don't always take time to notice the changing of seasons, a beautiful day, or the smile on our teenager's face.

*God of tranquility, remind me to pause from time to time in this busy world and sit in stillness, beholding all that you have created.*

It had been a very stressful week. I was working a lot of overtime, had a bad cold, and things were falling apart for my brother and his wife. My son was being particularly annoying this evening, clueless to all the stress I was feeling. Finally, I blew up at him, and acted irrationally and called him names. He retreated to his room, hurt and angry. Later, when I went to apologize, he said, "*Mom, I think you behaved very immaturely.*" And he was right.

The covenant we make with our teens is that we will maintain our composure and maturity, even in the face of our own stress—or their behavior. While we would like our children to "automatically know" when we are weary or when they need to give us some space, it's up to us to clearly define that need and take steps to fill it. Sometimes all it takes is a few minutes to recharge ourselves after a hectic week. Sometimes we have to ask ourselves if we are trying to do too much.

*Nurturing God, please help me to take care of myself when I am feeling stressed or sick, worried or tired, so that I can be a better parent for my teen. Guide me in finding solitary times with you in order to heal, rest, and pray.*

I'm wondering how well my son is fitting in at school. All the other boys his age are into sports and girls—things he isn't interested in at all. He's alone much of the time and just has one or two real friends. I'm worried that he's missing out on important parts of high school life, but when I ask him about it, he says it doesn't bother him at all and he's happy with his few, but close, friends.

Everyone has a different temperament and strengths. Some people are more naturally introverted, enjoying time spent with small groups of people—others are more outgoing. A part of good parenting is helping our children connect with others who may share their interests by giving them a gentle nudge in the right direction when necessary. Encouraging him to join a club or talking to the guidance counselor at his school may help if he doesn't appear happy. But if he does seem happy, it's best to just let him be himself.

*O God, please help my teen to continue to feel good about where he is in his development. Help him to reach beyond his comfort zone sometimes, so he can learn how to relate to many different types of people. And help me remember that he is his own person, with his own unique gifts and strengths.*

Yesterday we went shopping for the senior prom. My daughter narrowed her selection down to two very different dresses. One was low-cut, clingy, but not at all flattering, and somewhat inappropriate. The other was more elegant, really more a reflection of her personality. I could tell she felt conflicted, and was waiting for my reaction, but I didn't say a word—even though inside I was screaming, "No! Please! Not the low-cut one!" Later, after she had chosen the more elegant dress, she thanked me for letting her make up her own mind.

Our teens want us to trust their capability to make good decisions. If we don't overreact, they will usually choose what is best.

*O God, you believe in our ability to choose what is best for us. Help my teen move freely toward what is best for her, and remind me to stay out of her way when I can.*

A friend approached me yesterday because our daughters have stopped spending time together. Her daughter is experimenting with drugs, and my daughter isn't comfortable being around her as long as she is hanging around with "that crowd." Now her daughter's path is troubled, and my friend's eyes search mine for reassurance. A part of me wants to avoid dealing with the problem altogether. But then I think this could be *my* child! How would I want others to reach out to me?

It's difficult to watch a friend's child take an unhealthy path. We feel guilty and powerless, and afraid.

*Dear God, help me reach out to my friend with compassion and a willingness to listen, knowing that her family needs support and acceptance, not blame or rejection, during this frightening and insecure time.*

I could feel myself becoming heated. My daughter and I were about to engage in the same battle we've fought, oh, it seems a million times already. Then a change occurred within me and I thought, "I don't want to do this anymore. I don't have to." Quietly, I said these words to my daughter, and then I walked away. Later my daughter approached me, and we were able to have our first real discussion about this contentious topic.

We can get into negative downward cycles with our teens, increasing our efforts in the almost identical (and fruitless) pattern we have tried so many times before. Somehow, we end up hoping that this time the outcome will be different. In any relationship, it's important to remember that the only person we can truly change is ourselves.

*Holy Spirit, guide me toward the peaceful changes I need to make within myself, instead of always expecting my teen to change first.*

His friends have invited him to a girl/boy sleepover after the prom. We've told him *absolutely not*, that this isn't something we can support or condone in *any way*, but he's furious! He doesn't see anything wrong with it. He says *everybody* is going, and he has threatened to go with or without our permission.

It's important to have a discussion when the stakes are so high. Discussion is critical so that teens feel we are listening to them—and we feel that they are listening to us. Sometimes if we can really listen to our teens first, it can pave the way for honest dialogue and understanding. Why does he think we don't approve? What are we worried might happen? What is his plan? Would he allow us to contact the other parents? What sort of supervision will be present?

We need to explore all facets of the situation, knowing that in the end we don't have to agree to anything if we still feel uncomfortable, but that he will have to live with the consequences if he decides to go against our wishes.

*Dear God, it is so hard to be a parent sometimes! Why do I feel like I am the only one in my community who still has morals? This can't be true! God, please help me with these issues. Let me know when to relax my rules and when to hold fast. Help my older teen make prudent decisions.*

"If you had this need to begin with, give up your desire to be cool."

*Michael J. Bradley, Ph.D.*

Our children don't want us to be their friends. They have plenty of friends. What they need are parents: boring, predictable, homebody, God-loving parents.

We need to resist the desire to be a pal to our teens. We need to act maturely, and to dress in a way that reflects our age and values. We need to listen to our own music, not to abuse substances, and to make and enforce rules for acceptable behavior in our teens.

*O God, please help me to take the harder, oftentimes unpopular road of being a parent. Remind me that even though he won't admit it now, my teen will be forever grateful.*

I dropped my teen off at a party the other night. Although my daughter absolutely *hates* when I do this, I went to the door to meet the parents. No parent answered the door, but I could hear one of the girls yelling, "There's someone at the door!" as it opened and someone whisked my daughter inside.

The mother came to the door a few minutes later, wearing very tight jeans and short top—she looked to be about twenty-five! My heart sank, and all I could think of was how I was going to get my daughter out of there. But then something surprising happened. The woman remarked how most of the other parents hadn't even bothered to come to the door and thanked me for taking the time to introduce myself. Then we chatted for a few minutes. I felt so much better about leaving my daughter at her home.

Looks can be deceiving. It doesn't matter how much money a family has, or how upstanding they are in the community. These things don't make a good parent. What we really matters are the values we share about parenting our teens.

*O God, why does a part of me jump so quickly to judge others? Help me take the time to get to know the values of those who look or act differently–as well as those who act the same–to help to make my teen's world a safer place.*

"Some differences are bound to make us feel angry, isolated, and anxious at times, and for this reason it may be hard to keep in mind that differences are the only way we learn."

*Harriet Lerner*

How do I react when my teen presents a view that is different from mine? Do I look at it as challenging me? Or as a way to learn more about how he sees the world?

*Dear God, help me to respect my teen's attempts to form his own opinions, just as you respect my unique way of seeing the world.*

One minute she wants to sit next to me on the couch, instructing me to play with her hair; the next minute she freezes when I reach out to give her a hug. Some of the silliest things seem to reduce her to tears. She thinks she knows everything (except on the days when she's asking me for advice), and often she acts as if I'm the dumbest person ever to inhabit the world.

*All-knowing God, when this happens please whisper to me: "It's only a phase." Remind me to repeat this to myself as many times as necessary!*

After the recent news reports on child/teen abductions, my once secure, confident thirteen-year-old daughter is frightened to stay in the house by herself. I don't know what to tell her. I want her to know that bad things sometimes do happen, but I don't want her to be afraid all the time. Where is the balance between helping my child to be aware, but not overly frightened?

Most children have difficulties with the way the media can sensationalize current events. Even if an event occurs far away, children may over-identify with it, personalize it, or become "traumatized" by it, especially if a tragedy befalls a child near their own age. As parents, we must not allow reports of upsetting tragedies to saturate our families.

Sometimes, bad news will make its way to our doorstep. It can help if we teach our teens to carefully examine the negative messages, which may be feeding into their worries or fears. We can remind them that rarely will tragedy strike most of us. We can assure them that we are doing our best to keep them safe. We can guide them to pray for God's loving protection when they are feeling overwhelmed or insecure.

*All-protective God, show my teen how to calm down when worry threatens to overcome her. Help her to entrust herself to your safekeeping, O God. Please keep us safe from all harm.*

Graduation! I can't believe it's here. I've been so emotional all week; I just know I won't be able to stop crying at the ceremony. How mature they will look, bursting with pride, marching toward their future. So many choices, such excitement, such a time of growth and celebration!

The time of graduation is one of great joy and celebration. Truly, few events can make us prouder than watching our young adults as they ready themselves to enter the world.

*O God, thank you for the blessing, the joy, and the opportunity to celebrate this milestone with my child. We are so grateful that your everlasting love has brought us to this special place.*

"The pattern is unending: hello-goodbye-hello."

*Joyce Rupp*

I'm exhausted. A lot has been happening this month with graduation parties and her prom, and I'm suddenly feeling blue. What's next? Just the leaving, I guess, and already I can feel her beginning to pull away. "Wait!" I want to cry. "We still have all summer." But the writing is on the wall, and we know it. Things will never be the same. How will I ever bear to say goodbye?

We are constantly in a process of transition, growing into or out of phases with our children during the course of our lifetime. We are nearly always in a place of saying hello and goodbye to some part of them that we love.

*O Mary, you watched your one and only Son grow up, move out, and take his rightful place in the world. What worries you must have felt for him as he left his home with you to do the work of God. Remind me that I have survived all the other little good-byes of childhood. Let me know that you are with me, dear Mary, as I experience this next goodbye as my child goes out to take her rightful place in the world. And help me to welcome with joy that new hello of adulthood.*

"Whoever walks in integrity walks securely."
*Proverbs 10:9*

It is crucially important for us to have ourselves in order if we want to keep our teenager's respect and love. Now especially we must be scrupulous about our actions if we want our words to matter. A parent with an alcohol problem will have no credibility when he or she approaches his or her teenager about substance abuse; a parent stealing supplies from the office cannot hope to teach his or her child the importance of honesty.

*Help me walk in integrity, O God, so that my children will follow me toward the glory of you.*

# June

My daughter spends almost all of her time online chatting with friends. When I talk to other parents about this, they say it's typical. Their teens are doing the same thing. I guess our teens connect in ways we can't imagine. They know when someone has a problem or is in trouble much sooner than we do. I sometimes feel like I'm stumbling around in the dark, disconnected, with my head in the sand—and my daughter seems to like it that way!

Are we aware of our teens' subculture? Many communities are struggling with the influx of dangerous drugs: heroin, cocaine, marijuana, and ecstasy. Dating violence, sexual activity, binge drinking, and cigarette smoking are all a part of their world. Kids *do* know about these realities, and *may* tell us—if we know how to ask the right questions. Specific questions may yield a wealth of information!

*Guide me, O God. Open my eyes to the truth about the sub-culture my teen must navigate. Help me to stay connected to him, his friends, and our community. Help me to ask what I am afraid to ask. Help me hear what I am afraid to hear.*

Today my daughter asked me if I thought she looked fat. How can she say that? Her body is so beautiful! How I wish my skin still had that elasticity, that firmness. When I told her she was gorgeous, she just burst into tears. "You have to say that, you're my mother!" she cried.

Eating disorders can be triggered by a poor body image. Our children can "inherit" ways of thinking about dieting and food from us. Am I constantly saying negative things about my body? Am I dieting all the time? Do I talk about foods as being "good" or "bad"? Do I use certain foods as a reward?

We need to find ways to affirm our children's positive body image. We need to watch what we say about our own bodies in front of our teens. Our sons and daughters need to learn how to question the messages they get from society on the idea of body "perfection."

*O God, you have made us in your image, lovely and strong. Help us resolve to nurture our bodies, our beautiful temples, our wondrous gifts from you.*

Something isn't right. She looks thin. She's exercising all the time, wearing baggy clothes, picking at her food, only eating salads. Does she have an eating disorder? We've done everything to get her to eat more, but she only becomes angry. I thought we could handle this on our own, but now I wonder if we should do more.

Eating disorders are disorders of the mind, body, and spirit. Early intervention involving the entire family is crucial. We need to act before dysfunctional thinking patterns become entrenched or vital organs are affected. We need to learn about ways we can help our teens fight this dangerous disorder—it can be beaten, but it takes work.

*Dear God, don't let my fear, denial, or foolish pride stand in the way of getting my teen the help she needs. With your help, we can all recover from this serious problem.*

"Young women who eat compulsively have learned to use food as a drug that medicates away their emotional pain."

*Mary Pipher, Ph.D.*

Losing or gaining weight isn't the first sign that something is wrong—sometimes it is the *last* sign. Have we noticed we are missing large quantities of food? Is our teen more secretive about the food she consumes? Do we ever smell vomit after our daughter spends time alone in the bathroom? Does she suddenly want to exercise all the time?

I need to educate myself about all the signs of eating disorders and find out where to get assistance quickly if I suspect something is wrong.

*O God, I know that addictions and eating disorders can be diseases of denial. I am sometimes afraid to acknowledge what is right in front of me. Please open my eyes and reveal the truth. Knowing I can lean on you is what will sustain me through the difficult times ahead.*

Teenagers are always hanging around our house now. Their energy is kinetic, boundless. All they want to do is stay up late, watching each other play video games, laughing and talking into the wee hours of the night. I'm so tired—I just want my house back! I want to sit in my pajamas in front of the television or go to bed early if I feel like it, but I can't do that when they're around.

These days with my teens are fleeting. I need to stay in the "now," even during this hectic time. It is better to have them close, where I can keep an eye on them, than out "running the streets." One day our house will be silent, and I will wonder why I ever wished those voices away.

*O God, I know you want me to stay in the present. Soothe me when I am feeling tired, overwhelmed, or unsure of where my teen's needs end and my own needs begin. Help me find ways to connect with the teens coming into my home and provide adequate supervision so they can feel safe and have a good time.*

My son and a group of his friends wanted to have a graduation party at our house. I reminded them of the rules. There would be no drugs or alcohol. There would be supervision. We'd supply snacks and they could stay up all night if they wanted, but that was it. "Are you sure this is something you want?" I asked. "It might not be very exciting." They said, "Why do you think we want to have the party *here*? We want to be somewhere we can just have fun and not have to worry about any trouble."

*Thank you, dear God, for this blessing. Sometimes the rewards of parenting are so obvious I want to shout, "Alleluia!" I will bask in the moment of knowing that this time something has gone wonderfully, fabulously right.*

"Give me the children until they are seven and anyone may have them afterward."

*St. Frances Xavier*

Little children bring little problems. Big children bring...well, *big* problems. If we only knew then what we know now, we wouldn't have fretted so much over the small stuff when they were younger. It helps to remember that all of the lessons, values, and sense of faith that we instilled in our children as they were growing up are still there—to help them with the bigger problems they will face later in life.

*Help me, God, as my teen encounters the world with all its problems. Let us turn those big problems into manageable problems–together. When problems seem insurmountable to him, remind him that I will always be there for him, as you are always there for us.*

Tomorrow she is taking the test for her driver's license. She's so excited. I want to share that excitement with her, but honestly, I have alternately dreaded and looked forward to this day for so long that it's hard to figure out exactly *how* I'm feeling.

*Please God, protect her from all the possible dangers this new freedom will bring. Help me not to panic every time she is a few minutes late, imagining the worst. So much letting go, so much is out of my control! Sit with me in my extreme worry, God, so that I may know your soothing love.*

A boy from our high school died in a car accident over the weekend. Today was the funeral. Everyone was crying. No one could believe it! He was such a good kid. His future held such promise. So senseless! The shock of it has reverberated through our entire community. It's more than anyone can bear. We all will hold our children much closer during this very sad and tragic time.

*Merciful God, hear our prayers. Our hearts are breaking from this unspeakable loss. Give us the words that will help comfort our children and this boy's family. Help us remember to reach out to his family over the coming year, especially after everyone has moved on with their lives, when his family will need our continued support and care.*

"I could not be a poet without the natural world.... For me the door to the woods is the door to the temple. Under the trees, along the pale slopes of sand, I walk in ascendant relationship to rapture, and with words, I celebrate this rapture. I see, and dote upon, the manifest."

*Mary Oliver*

When we are close to nature and our surroundings, we are closer to God.

*O God, help me take the time to notice you in the natural world: in the fullness of a summer sky; in a smooth round stone lying at the bottom of a creek; in the sweet, celery-smell of freshly cut grass. Let the beauty of your creation restore my senses, and guide me ever closer to communion with you.*

"I will never get over this. Never! This is the worst thing that's happened to me in my whole entire life!"

Teenagers have an immediacy about them. They think that "this moment" will last forever, and they don't have the perspective that age and experience will eventually bring. Instead of jumping in to reassure them too quickly, it can help if we ask questions and foster their ability to figure out their options and calm themselves down. We can ask: "What other times in your life have you had to face obstacles? What did you do that helped? What can you tell yourself about this situation that might help you feel better?"

*Dear Lord, help me to foster self-reliance in my teen. Give her the strength to overcome the obstacles she encounters on her path. Help me to remind her of her past successes, and put this present difficulty in perspective. She needs to know that through the grace of your love for her, she can survive* anything.

My relationship with my mother has never been very close. She was always critical of me when I was growing up, and pre-occupied with her work and hobbies. I'm so afraid that my relationship with my daughter will become just as strained and distant, and that one day she won't want to spend time with me.

Every day we make choices whether or not to bring more love and intimacy into our relationships. It's important to regularly examine our actions: "What am I doing to nurture this relationship with my teen? How am I cultivating an atmosphere of mutual respect and shared interest that will follow us into her adulthood?"

*Gracious God, I want so much to be a good mother. As I deepen my relationship with my daughter, help me to also reach out to my own mother, sharing my hopes and fears, as you reach out to me all the days of my life.*

We've made an agreement. My daughter is all set for tomorrow, but something isn't sitting right with me. I feel like I've been "out-played, out-witted, out-lasted!" There's a pit of unease in my stomach about this decision, but I fear that if I change my mind now, I will lose all credibility with her.

True, we shouldn't make a habit of going back on our word, but there are times, especially when safety is an issue, when we *must* follow our instincts. How would we feel if we didn't change our minds and then the worst *did* happen?

*O Glorious God, help me as I struggle with these difficult issues of trust and letting go. Show me how to have conversations that preserve my teen's dignity, but also clarify my concerns.*

There is a picture on my desk of a trail leading to a mountain summit. The way to the top is steep and rocky, strewn with loose rocks and gravel. We hiked this trial last summer, almost turning back several times. Breathless and thirsty, we marveled at the view from the top, and congratulated each other on making it.

How do I handle it when things don't go quite the way I expected with my teen? It's easy to feel like giving up when we can't figure a way out of a situation. Sometimes we may distance ourselves from our teens with over-involvement in work or volunteer activities, because it hurts too much to acknowledge the lack of a connection. Even if we don't *physically* leave them, it can be a challenge not to *emotionally* abandon teenagers, just when they need us the most!

*Holy Lord, let me lean on you during times when I stumble, when my footing seems unsure. Let me be someone my teen can lean on. Even when the path gets rocky, help me stay close by his side.*

"I will try not to succumb to such conversation stoppers as, 'Dad, no teenager ever confides in her parents.'"

*Abigail H. Natenshon*

Have I stopped trying to talk with my teenagers because I assume that they don't want to talk to me? We have so much to offer from our unique perspective, yet many of us don't have confidence in our ability to connect. Many teenagers want to be able to confide in *both* of their parents. It may help to say, "What would make it easier for you to share important things with me? I want so very much to be a part of your world."

*God, my Father, you who listen to my every word, show me how to be patient, yet active in fostering a close and loving relationship with my teen.*

Every night we hear the sounds of teenagers roaring their cars up and down the street of our neighborhood. We hear them laughing too loudly, and wonder if they're getting into trouble with drugs, or drinking, or who knows what else. Our son isn't one of them, but what's to prevent him from joining them?

If teens decide to drink and do drugs their friends will not have to "force" them to do anything! By the time our children have reached their teenager years, we will have given them a set of values by providing them with a sound religious foundation, which will help guide most of their decisions. Teens are not unlike adults in the area of morals and values. Who they are *inside* will guide their behavior. For example, if our neighbor is cheating on his wife or his taxes, does that make it more likely that we will, too? Of course not! We keep our own Christian values, and gravitate toward people who feel pretty much the same.

*Holy Spirit, help my teen make decisions based on who he is, and not on who his peers are or who they may want him to be. Help him make decisions based on our Christian set of values, but if he should temporarily fall away from these values, let him know his faith will always be there for him, like a lighthouse, bringing him home to you.*

She wants to make all of her own decisions. She wants to stay out all hours of the night. "It's summer," she says. "I've graduated," she tells us, "and I'm eighteen!" Soon she'll be off on her own and we won't be able to stop her, so what are we to do?

We have the right to expect certain behaviors from our older teens, even when they reach adult-status. It is especially important at this stage to be able to negotiate compromises that address the needs of everyone in the household. That said, teenager's brains are still developing in the areas of logic and reason and will until they are in their mid-twenties! We need to help them balance their decisions with our experience and common sense.

*God, guide our family toward solutions that treat each person fairly, respectfully, and with consid eration and common sense.*

This afternoon, I teased my son about something. I couldn't resist. He's warned me that this is a sensitive topic for him, but I just went right ahead and teased him anyway. Maybe I did it because he had been distant with me this weekend, and I was just seeking some connection. Of course, he got angry, and now I feel so stupid. It completely defeated my purpose, pushing him further away instead of bringing him closer.

Teens have a low tolerance for teasing, especially since it is how the majority of their peers relate at this stage. As parents, we must realize that there will be times of silence and less connection. If we wait patiently and remain open, they will approach us eventually. It may not be on our timetable, but it *will* happen.

*Holy Spirit, help me be still and silent sometimes, especially when I feel my teens slipping away. Through the grace of your love, help them to find their way back to me.*

"You're trying to control me. You're stunting my growth. Get off my back already!"

Even though our teens may say these words, a part of them is secretly pleased that we care enough to set rules and limitations. Certainly, there are times to back off and give them some space. But if there are no boundaries, teenagers who have nothing to push against will eventually fall into that empty void of *nothing space* where there are no strong parents, no clear values, where they have to make all those decisions themselves—a dangerous and scary place indeed.

*Help me, O God, to feel secure about the boundaries I set with my teen. Show me how to be open to the process of negotiation, but to stand firm with the values I hold true.*

"...despite the influence of peer groups, adolescents themselves report that the most important relationship in their lives is still their parents."

*Ron Taffel*

When do I doubt my influence on my teenager? Have I given up trying to tell him what I believe about certain things? Do I buy into the myth that my teen's friends are more important than me?

*Father, help me to have confidence in the role I play in my teen's world. Don't let me give up on trying to be a part of his life.*

There's a different rhythm when they're out of school. Time is less structured. But I wonder what she's going to *do* with herself all summer. She says she has plans to baby sit, to find a part-time job. So far, she's mostly watched TV, chatted on the Internet, and talked on the phone. I'm afraid she will waste her entire summer.

Children, especially teens, grow more physically during the summer. They are sleeping more, resting more, and eating more, which allows their bodies to put more energy toward physical development. So, if they lounge around a lot and we think they're doing nothing, let's remember that they *are* doing something—they're growing.

*Dear God, help me not worry when my teens appear to be listless or lazy. They will have a lifetime of working and "doing" summers. For now, help me see that it's okay for them to just* be.

Our best friend's daughter is getting married. They've invited our whole family to the wedding. My older son refuses to go. He says he'd rather stay home than go to some "stupid" wedding. We're tempted to leave him behind; he can make our lives miserable when he's somewhere he'd rather not be.

Deciding which family events we would like our teenager to participate in is one of the trickier tasks of parenting an adolescent. Of course, we would like them to attend everything with us, just as they did before. They, on the other hand, seem to want nothing to do with us.

We need to encourage our teenagers to continue to participate in some family events, and allow them to pass on the ones that aren't as important to us.

*O God, help me as I try to balance the need for family connection with my teen's emerging need for independence. Fill me with the light of patience and understanding.*

**You're coming with us** 

Last week we decided to paint her room—no more little girl's pinks and purples, no more Barbie dolls on the shelves or stuffed animals on her bed. It's now a teenager's room with a desk to study at and posters of music stars hanging on the walls. Although it might sound silly, I started to cry when I passed by her redecorated room this morning.

There are so many reminders that our children are growing up. We pack away old toys or clothing that we know they will never use again. It can make us feel sad, but like pruning back a tree or shrub, we have to get rid of the old growth in order to make room for the healthy and new.

*O Mary, please show me how to delight in the healthy and normal development of my child. In your loving devotion to Jesus throughout his life here on earth, you exemplified a parent's struggle to balance loving and letting go, to accept gracefully the natural course of life and the will of God.*

"See, I am sending my messenger ahead of you, who will prepare your way...."

*Mark 1:2*

Who is preparing the way for my teen? Who takes an interest in him outside of our family? How do I feel about such relationships? Do I encourage him to spend time with the other adults in his life: coaches, youth ministry leaders, teachers, relatives, neighbors, and friends? Does he know how to keep himself safe?

*O God, you sent John the Baptist to prepare the way for our Lord, Jesus. Help me to encourage my teen to interact safely with the adults around him. They can help to guide him along life's path. Just as John the Baptist, they can help prepare his way toward you.*

We went to visit some friends in Vermont. Beautiful green mountains surround their little town. They live in a place they lovingly refer to as "the valley." A constant presence, those mountains, like arms around you, buffers from the rest of the world. It's easy to feel safe there.

Where does my teen go when she needs comfort? Do we have the kind of home she can come to for nourishment, peace, and sustenance? Or is our house often empty, everyone busy with their own schedules? How often do we leave her to fend for herself? Teens need to spend time with their friends, but they also need a safe place to come home to: a buffer from the rest of the world, where they can feel taken care of, protected, and beloved.

*O God, bless our home and all who reside here. Help us make it a place of comfort and nourishment where we can all find loving shelter.*

Last weekend my husband took our son and a few of his friends to a concert of their favorite rock band—loud music that I would definitely not want to sit though! They brought wax earplugs with them, along with snacks and drinks, and made plans for a sleepover afterward. And my husband—possibly the sweetest man on earth—was without a complaint, as if there was nothing he'd rather be doing then spending this time with his son.

*Dear God, thank you for showing me your love through my husband. His relationship with our son makes me want to be a better parent. You manifest your love for me through him in so many ways. Help me learn how to give the best of myself in return every day.*

"There's nothing wrong with teenagers that trying to reason with them won't aggravate."

*Anonymous*

How often do I get into senseless arguments with my teen? How often do I feel the need to have the last word? Maturity and experience can show us how to be gracious. All teens will argue just to argue—sometimes. All parents have the ability to keep their mouths shut—once in awhile!

Occasionally I may need to say, "You're right," or "You have an interesting point." Sometimes I may need to express my position with the fewest words possible, maybe even with no words at all.

*O God, in your silence I can learn so much about myself. When I am quiet, I can feel you gently nudging me toward my better self.*

I'm running around getting applications for my daughter's first job, taking her back for interviews, carting her back and forth to work at all hours. It's exhausting to shift my schedule to fit hers. Whose job is this, anyway?

Our teens' first job is another milestone in the journey toward independence. They really don't want to have to depend on us for transportation or support, but for now, they must.

*Jesus, in your humble beginnings as a carpenter, you teach us the value of an honest day's work. Help me not to resent the added chore of helping to introduce my teen into the world of work. Remind me how I felt about my first job, all the nervousness, and excitement, and pride it entailed.*

My son's got a summer job, but he's already been late twice! I've called his boss, inventing excuses for his tardiness. I yell at him every day to wake up and get going, but he acts as if he's doing everyone a big favor by rolling out of bed.

Some teens grow up with a sense of entitlement. They've gotten the message from us, or the media, or culture, that the world owes them. As parents, we aren't being helpful when we cover for them or shield them from responsibility.

*God, our Father, give me the strength to stand back and watch my teen fail sometimes.* Not *to protect him from failure and* not *shield him from natural consequences is difficult–but so necessary for his important transition into adulthood.*

The summer lies ahead of us, like a piece of ripened fruit, succulent, ready to bite! I have so many dreams about what I'd like to do—hiking, biking, camping—but when I share those ideas with my teenagers, they act annoyed, as if they would rather do *anything* other than spend time with me or our family.

If I want to spend a Saturday at a beach, hiking up a mountain, or kayaking in a lake, then it's best to do it sometimes—with or without my teen. At other times I need to drag them along as part of a family adventure, as something that's "good for their soul."

*Dear God, help me to know when to venture out by myself, and when to bring my family along. I know that you always yearn to have me closer, as you pull me out into the beauty of this world. Sometimes I can leave my family behind, and trust that gentle "tug" which is telling me you want to spend some time alone with me!*

# July

I suggested to my teens that we go to a nearby farm to pick berries today, which, of course, was met with great resistance. Only the promise of two blueberry pies for dessert and a few dollars each got them into the car. Once we arrived at the farm, they had a contest to see who could fill their baskets first. We picked more than enough berries for pies. I bought them each a soda from the ice-chest by the checkout stand. They spent the ride home laughing, eating berries, and bragging about who picked the most berries.

It's okay to bribe our teens occasionally to get them to do something. Rarely will they participate willingly if they perceive an activity as being "not cool."

*Help me, God of new beginnings, to realize we have entered yet another new phase where I may need to do more to convince my teens to do things with me. Help me invent new and creative ways to bring them closer to each other and to you.*

A hotly contested Wiffle Ball tournament took place in our yard today. There was lots of yelling and shouting of the rules. Deep voices broke the occasional silence—the voices of almost-men playing not boys. Then a time-out, when they consumed gallons of soda and packages of hot dogs in a matter of minutes!

What joy to have a back yard full of energetic voices on a summer afternoon!

*Thank you God, for the grace of this fleeting pleasure, for this afternoon when voices rang through the air and your love for me was overflowing.*

Every day, it seems, I do something wrong. I say the wrong thing or look at her the wrong way or I'm wearing something wrong. How can one person have so much *wrong* with them?

I remember when we were growing up, we used to give my mother a hard time when she mispronounced a word. It was a little thing that we could've let slide, but we pounced on her immediately, as if it were somehow a reflection on us when she said a word the *wrong* way. Or maybe we were thinking that we finally knew more than she did.

*O God, please remind me of my own adolescence during times when I am confused and hurt by my teen's behavior. Help me not to take these criticisms personally, but to see them as moments of defining her "self" as separate from me.*

This afternoon our family went to our town's annual Fourth of July parade, complete with marching bands, fire engines, and World War II veterans. Our teenager was bored; he had places to go, friends to meet. "Can't we leave now?" he asked, repeatedly. We told him to spend the rest of the parade thinking about the meaning of the words "independence and freedom." He told us that he wanted the *independence* to decide when he could get *freedom* from this parade! We laughed, but then had a wonderful conversation on the way home.

Independence and freedom. Any adolescent can relate to these topics. Our teens are developing opinions about more worldly issues, and it can be fascinating to hear their views. If we give them a chance, discussions about the world can be a wide open window to their ever-expanding minds.

*O God, help me to find ways to bring deeper meaning into our experiences and conversations with my teen, and to discuss ideas and values on a regular basis with him.*

My daughters are fighting with each other again over insignificant things. They were almost best friends at the start of the summer, when everything was new. Now, I guess boredom is setting in and they have nothing better to do than pick on each other. I am so tired of it. It seems that I'm always yelling at them to stop bickering!

Being with each other all day long instead of busy at school or with planned activities is yet another challenge for our teens. Do they need help in structuring their free time? Do they need to spend some time apart?

I may need to help my teens make some kind of plan of how they're going to spend their days. I may need to help them learn the tools they need for negotiation and compromise with each other. They need to know that I will give them my full attention when I am finished with my task, but that they must also learn to work out their differences themselves when I am preoccupied.

*O God, give me patience when I feel myself getting angry at my children's squabbles. Help me look toward solutions that can move us in the direction of peace in our home.*

"O God...my soul thirsts for you;
my flesh faints for you,
as in a dry and weary land
where there is no water."

*Psalm 63:1*

Where do I go when I am thirsty for God? What regular spiritual practice do I have that brings me closer and deeper to the Lord? How often do I read Scripture, meditate, or write in a journal? Where do I go for guidance? Do I have a trusted friend who is spiritually "grounded"? Would they help show me the way?

*O Precious God, come closer, I am thirsty for your love. My heart is open and anxious to be filled with your glory.*

My friend worries about boys taking sexual advantage of her daughter. She's noticed that her daughter's body has begun to develop and that the phone has been ringing more lately, with deep voices on the line asking for her teen. "Parents of boys don't understand," my friend says. "They're lucky they don't have to worry about all of this!"

Today, none of our teens are safe from society's pressures to engage in premarital sexual activity. I tell her that I worry as much about my sons as I do my daughters.

How often do we stereotype by gender, worrying more about certain issues for our daughters and others for our sons? All of our children, boys and girls, are vulnerable in ways that most of us can't comprehend unless we begin to understand their culture. We must have open conversations with our teens about the pressures they may face to have sex, and how to deal with those pressures. We need to remind them about the sacredness of the sacrament of marriage, and the importance of chastity as an integral part of Christian life.

*Dear God, I know that you love all of our children and want to keep them safe. Please open my eyes and show me how and where I can be most helpful in keeping them pure and close to you.*

This morning she started soccer camp. Most of her friends were there practicing when I dropped her off at the field. I stood there watching for a few minutes. Hot and sweaty, they galloped down the field, so intent, so confident, and so able. I never had the opportunity to play competitive sports; a part of me watched in awe.

*I praise you, God, for allowing my daughter to have the chance to know the joy of moving her body, the thrill of competing, and the importance of working with others as a team. Thank you for these opportunities for her to grow toward her fullest potential.*

He's off to camp today. Two weeks of working at a wilderness camp for him and two weeks of freedom for me! This is the true beginning of my summer vacation. I don't have to cook special meals, wash his huge piles of laundry, or listen to him telling me how bored he is. I feel a little guilty for feeling like this, but I'm kind of happy that he's gone!

It's okay to feel joyful when we get a break from taking care of our loved ones. Parenting a teen can be emotionally and physically exhausting. Maybe it's supposed to be that way, so that when they do grow up, we can somehow find joy in the "letting go" of our teen.

*Gracious Lord, allow me to enjoy the gift of this time away from my teen without feeling guilt. Help me use this time wisely, to replenish myself and come closer to you. Remind me to continue taking better care of myself when my teen comes home again.*

Tonight we went to a nearby park for an outdoor concert. We brought only a blanket with us, and happy anticipation. We weren't disappointed. What is it about music soaring through the warm air of a summer's evening that makes us feel so good inside?

Music reaches into our very souls. It connects us to something bigger and deeper, to our humanness, and to the God who created us.

*Thank you, God, for the gift of music in my life. To be able to hear your love for me expressed through sweet evening song is a joyous blessing.*

I overheard my daughter's friend saying that it's okay to be "friends with benefits." Another time I heard them describing a boy as "straight edge." I only catch snippets of their conversations. What do these phrases mean? I don't want to seem intrusive by asking, and maybe they wouldn't tell me anyway.

As parents of teens, we need to try to keep abreast of the current slang. Important information is sometimes communicated in "code," and this code is always changing. "Friends with benefits" means that casual sex may take place without commitment or love. "Straight edge" means that the person doesn't use drugs or alcohol. If we feel uncomfortable asking our teens about their slang, other parents or a school counselor can be valuable interpreters.

*Father, help me to seek out information when I'm feeling in the dark, and light the way toward a better communication with my teen.*

One morning, my neighbor told me she was at her wit's end trying to deal with her son. The next week she announced she read a terrific book, which helped put the whole situation in perspective.

When is the last time I read a parenting book? Was it when my child was in diapers? We don't have to figure out everything for ourselves or feel alone with our problems. Reading about how others have handled similar issues can be comforting and illuminating. In this fast-paced era, we need as much information as we can get about the perils and pitfalls of adolescence.

*O God, help me to seek out information when I am feeling overwhelmed. Direct me to a source that is clear and accurate. Help me to find comfort and reassurance in Scripture.*

A parent told me about all the volunteer work her teen is amassing this summer. I asked if her daughter is enjoying it. She replied, "No, she's miserable, but we have to have something to put on the college application—she just *has* to get into a good school."

How much pressure do we put on our teens to get into a "good" college? When they end up doing things to satisfy someone else's idea of what is important, those activities lose their intrinsic worth. Some teens naturally want and need to be busy, but many of today's teens run themselves ragged trying to outdo each other in sports and civic activities. They end up losing a part of their childhood, and are burned out before they even begin college.

*Jesus, please help my teen to say "no" sometimes to activities, even when everyone around her is saying "yes."*

I'm constantly searching my son's room for evidence, although he's done nothing wrong. I smell his breath when he comes home, look in his pockets before I do the laundry, and drive by the places where he says he'll be. I want to catch him *before* anything terrible happens.

For some of us, trust is extremely difficult. Yet, our overly suspicious behavior could send the message that we don't trust our teens. Unfortunately, they may decide that they might as well live "down" to our expectations. No matter what we do, we can't be with our teens all the time. Somehow, unless we have reason to believe otherwise, we have to begin to trust them. There will be many signs if something isn't right, and usually plenty of opportunities to act if that trust is broken.

*Lord, help me to trust my teen, just as you, O God, have always trusted me. He needs my trust in order for him eventually to learn to trust himself, and to trust in your love and wisdom.*

"Each of us needs to withdraw from the cares which will not withdraw from us. We need hours of aimless wandering, or spates of time sitting on park benches, observing the mysterious world of ants and the canopy of treetops."

*Maya Angelou*

Since our teens are so self-absorbed and focused on pleasure, they can serve as reminders when we aren't taking good care of ourselves. Instead of feeling resentful at their self-indulgence, perhaps we can learn from them. When was the last time I sat on a park bench or did some aimless wandering? When did I last find solace in the quiet comfort of the Lord?

*God, help me learn from my teen to take time out from my busy world to enjoy the pleasures of every season. You yearn for us to notice every living thing you have created and to spend time basking in your blessings.*

Late this evening I went for a walk. It was a warm, sultry night. The fireflies were out, and a full, almost lemon-colored moon hung in the sky between the trees. I didn't need a jacket as I walked, listening to the call of crickets and the barking of a dog. It was perfectly warm and delicious, and even the thought of cool sheets couldn't beckon me back inside.

Somehow, God finds us on these nights and brings us outside with him.

*Help me absorb your wonderful summer nights, O God. Breathing in your warm summer's breath, let us walk together on these evenings, just the two of us, like old friends.*

A thunderstorm blew through this afternoon. It made a big ruckus, with hail as big as marbles. Then, in a matter of minutes, it seemed the storm was gone.

The storms of my daughter's adolescence are passing more quickly now. It takes almost no time at all for her to pull herself out of a bad mood, when before it seemed to take days. Her comments to those around her are kind and generous. She's offering to help us with chores. It's delightful to be around her, watching her become a mature person.

*O God, the Bible is full of stories about the return of someone who has gone astray. It gives us hope in your renewing love. Thank you, Lord, for bringing my gentle daughter home to me.*

It's so hot outside! We're in the middle of an oppressive heat wave. None of us slept well last night. The morning air outside is already stifling, and we're all more than a bit crabby. Snapping at each other over the least thing, we've grown careless with what we do or say to one another.

*Dear God, help us when we are overheated to slow our pace. Help us to be tender, loving, and kind to those whom we love the most, and to show our love for you by loving each other.*

He's run off to swim with friends. He's driving them to a nearby beach. He's only had his license for a few months, but already he's responsible for other kids' lives, too. Another set of worries! Will he drive carefully? Will they remember to wear their seat belts? Should I have let them go at all? This driving thing is so big and scary. I wonder how I'll ever get through it!

*Holy Spirit, please watch over my teen. Terrible things can happen so easily. With the grace of your love, help him accept this new responsibility and handle it with vigilant care.*

Late last night I caught my son on the couch downstairs with his girlfriend. They were both in a state of undress, mortified by my sudden intrusion. It was an uncomfortable moment, to say the least, but I controlled my reaction and calmly asked him to bring her home. When he returned, we had the best talk we'd had in months. I told him how I had waited until marriage to engage in sexual activity, how I'd never regretted my decision. He shared with me the pressures he'd felt, how it seemed like "everyone" was doing it. We explored what our religion says about premarital sex, all the emotional, spiritual, and physical dangers of sexual activity without the bond of marriage, and the reasons why these teachings exist.

It's important to stay calm during unexpected moments, especially with our teens. Our calmness gives them a chance to reflect on their own behavior instead of immediately reacting with defensiveness. It can open up the moment to emotional connection and healing.

*O God, please fill the room with calmness during the unexpected moments of adolescence. Help me calmly discuss with my teen those actions which could have a lifetime of consequences.*

"All girls need help making sense of the sexual chaos that surrounds them. As opposed to what they learn from the media, they need to be told that most of what happens in relationships is not sexual."

*Mary Pipher, Ph.D.*

When was the last time I sat and watched a "love scene" in a movie or a sexualized music video with my daughter and then talked about it afterward? Parents have to give strong messages about moral values to counter-act what our teens are bombarded with every day from media and their peers. We need to begin to have these conversations at an early age, before they begin to tune us out.

*God, help my voice become stronger during these turbulent times. I need to be more than a blip on my teen's radar screen in order to get my message across.*

I've started going through menopause. Crazy symptoms like night sweats and insomnia; my heart feels like it's beating out of its chest. I've been short-tempered with my husband and the kids. And my teenaged daughter, with her developing body, is full of her own up-and-down hormonal changes. How are we ever going to survive these changes at the same time without killing each other?

God must have some sense of humor, moving mothers into mid-life at the same time their teenagers are becoming sexually mature.

*Help me laugh at life's ironies, O Lord. Guide me to accept this new phase of my life. Remind me to seek out solutions when my symptoms feel unmanageable.*

She wanted to bring a friend along on our annual vacation. She begged and pleaded, "But there will be nothing for me to do." Finally, we relented, but it makes everything so different from previous years. The girls go off on their own, pretending they're not with us.

How I long for those vacations when she was still a small child. Our family felt so close then, just us against the world. Now the whole world is beating down our doorstep, and try as we might, we can't keep it out!

*Holy Mary, please help us to know when to bring the world into our family, and when we must insist on pure and simple "family" time.*

My son's rock band has spent most of the summer practicing in our garage. Finally, the big day arrived: they decided they were ready to perform a "concert" for some neighborhood kids. They were nervous all afternoon, rehearsing for those last few hours. After dinner, the kids began to take their places on the lawn in front of our house. About two dozen kids, all ages and sizes came clapping and cheering, to listen to our four young musicians at their first live performance.

*Dear Father, I thank you for this day when my teen could shine. Thank you for the other kids who simply showed up and listened. Thank you for the gift of memory, so that we will never forget this wonderful summer evening.*

It's been a yearly ritual for our family to spend a few days of the summer in a tiny cabin by the lake. Suddenly, the day before we were supposed to leave, our seventeen-year-old announces he's old enough to stay home alone. He doesn't want to come with us, and besides, he told us, he's found out he has to work. "Go on, ahead," he said, smiling confidently, "I'll be just fine."

How do we know when they're old enough to be left behind? What part of us is truly concerned about their capabilities? What part of us mourns this transition and doesn't want to let them go?

*Holy Mary, how did you manage when Jesus began to go off on his own, apart from your family? It must have filled you with sadness and worry, but also a twinge of pride. Please help me to remember that this independent phase, too, is a necessary part of growing up, and with the grace of God our teen is growing his way toward adulthood.*

She complains that we treat her unfairly. She thinks that her younger sister gets to do things at a much earlier age. She says we push her harder because she's the oldest. I guess we do treat them differently, but that's only because they *are* so different!

While one teen handles the responsibility of working and keeping up grades, another might fall apart. While one teen may be able to balance an active social life and schoolwork, another may need stricter curfews. One myth about parenting is that we must treat all of our children exactly the same. We do need to convey that no matter what, we love each of them equally for being uniquely and wonderfully themselves. But since they have different needs, we need to adjust the rules accordingly.

*Heavenly Father, help us to know that it's okay to treat each child differently; it doesn't mean we love them any less. You love all of your children with the same vastness of compassion and tender pride. Help us to always model you for our children.*

I'm running around packing and doing laundry and making sure we're all set to go. My kids are sitting around, like they always do, leaving everything up to me. What's wrong with this picture? I'm angry and resentful before we even get out the door—not a great way to start a vacation.

Many times the packing and planning for a vacation falls on one person. It's important to enlist help from our children at each phase of their lives, especially when they are older and able to do more. Give each of them a packing list and chores to do. Initially, it may take more time to delegate these jobs, but it's well worth the effort to teach them responsibility and reduce our own stress level.

*Dear God, please help me to ask for help from my family whenever I am feeling overwhelmed.*

Finally, our vacation is here! All this time together—just our family. No friends or jobs or activities or sports or phone or TV or computer...nothing to distract us from being together! So why are we fussing at each other and arguing? Why is it suddenly so hard to be together?

Whenever our family vacations together, we seem to have to get to know one another all over again. We each handle the excitement and transition to "vacation-mode" so differently. Some of us want to race to every activity, others just want to sit and relax, but, with a bit of planning and compromise, everyone's needs can be satisfied.

*O God, please bless this time we have together as a family. Help us scale down our expectations. Remind us to spend time together as well as apart, as "vacation" will mean different things to each of us. Let this be a time of renewal and joy for all of us as a family.*

What a wonderful vacation! I haven't relaxed this much in months...maybe even years. We lingered over breakfast and went for leisurely walks. We played simple family games, and we laughed a lot. It was as if we had all the time in the world—and we did. Now I have to return to my busy life, and it makes me sad. I wish it didn't have to end.

What are some things we can do at home to de-stress and connect with one another regularly? Can we take walks together sometimes? Can we have family game night or some other activity once a week and stick to it? Can we sit down together as a family and pray before our evening meal, asking for God's love and blessing? Can we establish time for family prayer each day?

*Dear God, remind me to build a little "vacation" into every day. Living in the moment is something that takes practice. In this busy world, it can be difficult to make time to relax and worship you through the daily connection of love and time spent with my family. But help me to remember that this is always possible, if I make it a priority.*

Cell phones. Beepers. E-mail. Computers. Video games. TV. So many electronic devices, all designed to keep us connected to each other. So why do most of us feel so *dis*connected from one another?

Am I spending too much time on the phone or computer when my family is around? Do I use the cell phone constantly when I'm in the car or when I'm at an event where I should be paying attention to what's going on around me? Do I monitor how long my teens spend on the computer or playing video games?

We need to pause during our daily schedule and ask: How do I remain spiritually and emotionally connected to the ones I love? How do I help my family "plug" into each other's love?

*O God, help me occasionally to step away from this busy, modern world. Remind me to bask in my children's laughter and voices, and to gaze into the face of my spouse. You want us to love and cherish each other. Show our family how to slow down and re-connect through the grace of your love.*

How did another summer month pass by so quickly? We're more than halfway through summer, and already my thoughts turn to fall. Suddenly I feel summertime slipping away, yet there's so much more I want to do. I haven't yet gone for an evening picnic in the park or spent a day at the beach, and the hammock in our backyard sits empty most of the time.

How can we keep that laid back feeling of "summer" in our grasp? In this busy time of parenting teens, we need to schedule our leisure activities as much as we schedule everything else. If we don't write it on a calendar, it just might not happen. It can help to prioritize a list of summertime activities, and remind ourselves that chores and projects can wait.

*O God, Creator of this beautiful world, help me to delight in your gift of summer and to take the time to do the things that give me summertime joy.*

# August

## *August 1*

"The fruit of silence is prayer;
the fruit of prayer is faith;
the fruit of faith is love;
the fruit of love is service;
the fruit of service is peace."

*Mother Teresa*

Do I engage in activities that are bearing fruit in my life? Which ones nourish me in my spiritual journey? Which ones empty or drain me?

*Dear God, help me to know that the fruits of spirituality are mine whenever I choose to come to your table.*

I was on the phone talking to my sister this morning. I was complaining about how lazy my daughter has been this summer, wondering where she gets those "lazy genes." My sister started to laugh. "Don't you remember how you spent your summers as a teenager? Watching soap operas and lolling in the pool!"

Oops! Sometimes we need a gentle reminder of what we were like when we were growing up to help us understand how our teens are more like us than we realize.

*Holy God, remind me of the pleasures of carefree days and peaceful nights. How fleeting and wonderful they were. Don't let me begrudge my teen the wonders of her youth; there will be time enough for her to enter that crazy world of adulthood. Bring her closer still to you, as she enjoys these years of her life.*

Our child complains that our neighbor's daughter is treating her poorly. They have been best friends for years, but suddenly this girl is excluding our daughter from shopping trips and the other activities they once enjoyed together. Apparently, she now has a new best friend. I'm angry that this parent doesn't seem to be doing anything to encourage her daughter to include my daughter in all the fun!

Children move in and out of relationships with their neighborhood friends. It's important for parents to interfere as little as possible with those squabbles, but to communicate when real issues erupt. At times, nothing we do can help, and we just have to help them agree to coexist peacefully. Some teens will rediscover their childhood friends later on, wondering how they ever drifted apart.

*Loving God, help me to understand and appreciate my neighbor, and not expect that we can fix our children's friendship. Please help my daughter to deal with the very real pain of a lost friendship. Help her to move on to other relationships that will bring her joy. Help her to recognize that you are her ever-faithful friend.*

Yesterday, at the grocery store, I ran into the parent of one of my daughter's friends. My husband and I had been talking about how polite this girl is whenever she visits our home. I was already late for an appointment, but something made me stop and share with this mother our impressions of her daughter. "Well, I'm glad somebody sees that side of her," she said, laughing with relief. "I'm so glad you said something nice about her, she's been giving me such a hard time lately."

We all need to hear wonderful things about our teens because they can sometimes be showing us their worst at home!

*Dear Lord, help me to never pass up the opportunity to say something nice about someone else's child; it may be what they desperately need to hear during a difficult time.*

This morning, as I was walking along the beach, the water was quiet and calm. It was so peaceful. Watching the gulls and cormorants feeding by the jetty, I became mesmerized by the light glinting off the water. Suddenly, a few rogue waves began to strike the shore, lapping loudly against the rocks with a persistent rhythm. It was as if God were beside me saying, "I am here. Notice me. I am here."

How often do I really notice my teen? Do I truly see him and all that he is becoming, or do I often focus on something else? Sadly, it's easier to pay attention when problems arise, rather than notice the wonder of our teen during calm and peaceful times.

*Dear God, help me to notice you in all things and in all places. Help me to notice how wonderful my teen truly is.*

My boss is talking about downsizing. He's warned me to be prepared for the worst. I haven't said a word to anyone at home. We barely have enough to send my oldest off to college next year. We really need my additional income. Why *now*? Why *me*? What am I going to do? I feel so vulnerable, weak, and ashamed.

We forget during our moments of fear and desperation that others can offer us support, encouragement, and love. It's important to not carry our burdens alone. There are always solutions, even if they are not evident at the time.

*Dear God, help me to share my fears and concerns with those who love me. Help me to have the courage to deal with this life-changing event and to see the possibilities and opportunities that may still lie hidden from me.*

My husband wants our son to put all of his hard-earned money into the bank for college. I think he should contribute to some of his expenses at home, like gas for the car. Yesterday we had a big argument over this, and we hardly ever fight.

Money can be a difficult issue. In our society, there are no easy answers in deciding how much teens need to contribute to the family. If we routinely set aside money for saving, money for giving, and money for spending, it's easy to show him how to develop a budget. But if we are continually in debt and spending beyond our means, then the issue of money can become emotionally loaded, taking on a life of its own.

*Generous God, help me to examine my relationship to money. Remind me whenever I find myself overreacting to any problem that there may be deeper issues to explore.*

"As a deer longs for flowing streams,
so my soul longs for you, O God."

*Psalm 42:1*

What is my soul longing for? When did I last nourish that deeper part of me that longs for connection to something greater than myself? What do I need to do to fill that need? What nourishes the soul of my teen? Can I help her to identify what she is longing for?

*Help me to connect more deeply to you, O God. And guide my teen toward what is truly nourishing for her soul, so that she may find refreshment in communion with you, now and forever.*

She wanted me to take her to the mall. "Come on. It'll be fun," she said.

Fun? How could anyone ever describe shopping with a teenaged girl as *fun*? She found a pair of shoes she liked in the first store, but then we had to check every other store in the mall to make sure that *those shoes* were the ones she really, *really* wanted. We stopped for a snack halfway through, and she surprised me by saying, "I know I'm being kind of a pain about these shoes. And I know you don't really like shopping, but, well...thanks for loving me enough to do this." And suddenly, this shopping trip with her became a hundred times more than just fun!

We never know when a golden moment with our teen will arise, moving our relationship to a deeper level, moving us closer to them and to God. What we do know is that if we don't spend time together, these golden moments have no chance of occurring at all.

*Thank you, dear God, for this gift of being able to spend time with my teen. Help me to continue to find ways to show her the depth of my love for her.*

Today is my birthday. I have to think twice these days to figure out how old I am—or maybe I don't really want to remember. The way I usually remember is by adding thirty years to my son's age. So that means I'm...no, wait, that can't be! How can I be turning...?

Why do some of us approach the aging process with such dread and trepidation rather than with joy and celebration? Birthdays in mid-life become such milestones. Each year our birthdays push us farther away from our youth and closer to the generation that came before us.

*Dear God, help me grow into mid-life with optimism and grace, so that my teen will know the beauty, the wisdom, and the joy that comes with aging.*

I shared with my best friend all the things about my daughter that had been pushing me "right over the edge." My friend burst out laughing and said, "Well, that sort of sounds like somebody else I know." I glared at her. "What are you trying to say?"

She isn't like me. She can't be like me! I was never like that! Well, okay, maybe...a little. Why are the things we dislike so much in our children so often the very things we dislike or fear about ourselves? By encountering the parts we don't like about ourselves in our teens, we can learn how to forgive and embrace the parts of us that we'd rather wish away.

*O God, you made us wholly human, and you love us–warts and all! Show me how to love all of myself, so that I can embrace and love all of my teen.*

One of my favorite pictures in our family room is a photograph of my son as a toddler, intently examining a seashell while sitting on a beach blanket. In the background, caught quite by accident, is a teenager running toward the ocean with a surfboard. I remember first seeing that picture and gasping—would my little baby ever really turn into a big, scary teen? How far away his teenage years seemed then and yet how quickly they have arrived!

Some experiences of the toddler years are revisited as our children become teenagers. We can see the same seeds of separation and defiance that marked the "terrible twos." Once again, our children feel an urge to assert themselves and to say, "No!" It's no wonder we sometimes feel the need to say: "Stop acting like a two-year-old!"

*O God, help me to recognize that it will be difficult for both my son and me to prepare for the looming separation of his child-self from his adult-self. Help me to be there for him, even when he's acting like a two-year-old. May I be ready to embrace the independent person he is in the process of becoming.*

"Parents can help by listening to their daughters, who need as much parent time as toddlers. Teenagers need parents available when they are ready to talk."

*Mary Pipher Ph.D.*

When was the last time I dropped whatever I was doing to be available for my teen? When was the last time that I fully concentrated on what she had to say? When I find myself getting bored by her rambling stories, usually I only have to wait a few minutes before the real issue comes bounding to the surface. I feel as if she is testing me with all this small stuff to see if I am truly listening.

*Loving God, help me to be there to listen whenever, and however, she chooses to share with me, as you are always there ready to listen to me.*

I always rush to her side whenever she has a problem, and I try to help her solve it. Our family hasn't had it easy. She used to appreciate my advice, but lately she seems resentful. Nothing I say seems to help, and she gets angry with me for trying.

Our teens are developing the tools they need to help themselves, independent of us. We don't need to provide all the answers. Sometimes, it may be better to just ask, "What is your plan? What do you think would be helpful right now?"

*O God, the next time I find myself rushing in to solve a problem for my teen, help me to ask what she thinks* she *should do about it first.*

My cousin's daughter has just entered drug rehabilitation for the third time. One more arrest and she's going to go to prison. She's addicted to heroin, and our family is completely spent with insurmountable feelings of loss and despair.

*O Mary, you know that there is no greater loss to endure than the loss of one's child. Please help those who have lost a child to death, drugs, or despair. Our sadness seems endless. Let us find hope and peace in your loving example. Show us the way to move through our grief toward the promise of inner peace.*

"For wisdom is better than jewels,
and all that you may desire cannot compete with her."

*Proverbs 8:11*

Where do I look for wisdom? Who walks beside me to show me the way? Do I sometimes feel so baffled and helpless in dealing with my teen that I shut down and stop looking for solutions?

*God of wisdom, help me to read Scripture, and to seek out spiritual guidance and parenting wisdom from others who can help me when I am feeling lost. Help me to trust more in my own wisdom and experience, which is truly a gift from you.*

This morning I loaded our kayak on the back of my car and drove to the lake near our home. I dragged it down to the water. I almost tipped getting in! But, finally settled, with oar in hand, I slowly paddled across the lake. The sun was sparkling off the rippling water—it was gorgeous. I carefully marked in my mind's eye my "put-in" spot; the shoreline looked so different from the boat.

When did I last try something new and different? When did I last look at a problem from a different vantage point? When dealing with teens, we often become locked into a single point of view. It can help if we try to expand our vision, perhaps by looking at the problem from their perspective.

*God of replenishment and rejuvenation, help me to "row away" from my problems occasionally, so that I can return to them with a fresh perspective.*

My daughter has agonized over her college essay and written at least a dozen drafts. She says it needs to be *perfect*. She's a perfectionist in other areas too, becoming disturbed if her books or belongings are out of order. And she's overly concerned about cleanliness when we go out to eat. In fact, she's worrying all the time! I try to reassure her, but nothing I say seems to help.

For some teens, perfectionist tendencies or excessive worry can be signs of obsessive-compulsive disorder or other anxiety disorders. Repetitive thoughts and worries are warning signs that something isn't right. When reassurance doesn't work, it might help to open a conversation: "Tell me about what this is like for you. I'd like to know more about your suffering."

*Soothing God, help me have the conversation with my teen that may lead to clarity for both of us. Guide me toward appropriate help for my teen when my instincts tell me that something is not right.*

Last night my daughter's friends brought her home early from a party. She said that at the party she had suddenly started feel dizzy, to sweat, and to shake. Her heart felt like it was bursting out of her chest. She felt like she was "going crazy." I asked her if she had taken anything, drugs...*anything*...or if someone had put something into her drink. She said no, and then she confessed that this wasn't the first time she felt this way. She thinks she was having a panic attack.

Panic attacks can occur in the teenage years, most often to girls. As parents, we may sometimes deny the severity of the symptoms. We might tell our teens to work harder at fighting the feeling, or that it will go away if they just ignore it. Sometimes symptoms do eventually diminish, but most of the time they will persist without some kind of treatment. Unfortunately, the longer symptoms go untreated, the more entrenched they may become.

*Heavenly Father, there is something seriously wrong with my teen, something she can't control. I am afraid for her. Please show us the way to her healing.*

"Love is unconditional for babies and puppies. After that, unfortunately, love is a two-way street."

*Anonymous*

Our fifteen-year-old treated us all like dirt over the weekend: neglecting his chores, teasing his sister, snapping at me. It got so bad that I wanted to do nothing for him. *Nothing*. When he asked me to drive him to his friend's house that evening, I refused. Then I told him he could get his own dinner, too, and I went upstairs to take a bath.

Our teens need to learn that in the real world, if you treat people badly, they will likely respond in the same way. They may not continue to love you, take care of you, or want to make things right. Many times, they will simply walk away.

*O God, show me when I need to walk away from my teen's bad behavior so he will learn how to treat others with kindness and consideration. Help me to teach him to walk in your ways.*

"A powerful myth prevails in girls lives, namely, that popular girls have all the fun. In fact, the popular girls are often the most at risk of losing their authentic selves. They are the most insecure in their social positions, competing daily—often desperately—to be included and stay on top."

*Rachel Simmons*

Where does my daughter fit in the social order? Is she constantly worried about fitting in? How does she feel about being popular? Who are the popular girls? What are they like? How do they treat others in the class? Do they have to be mean or "fast" to stay popular?

It's important for our teens to have a strong sense of self and an understanding of interpersonal behavior that they can carry with them throughout their life. There are many good books which we can read with our teens, so that they can be more prepared to deal with the cultural phenomena of cliques and popularity.

*Holy Mother of God, help me to have this conversation with my daughter. Help her to be kind and inclusive toward others and to forgive the meanness of her peers. Let me teach her to use your commandment of love as a guide for her behavior toward others.*

One afternoon I remarked to my son that one of his friends seemed like such a nice boy, and wondered aloud why my son hadn't invited him over in a while. Imagine my surprise when he told me that they hadn't been friends for a long time, and that this boy had become one of the biggest drug dealers in the school!

One of the reasons why we shouldn't try to pick our children's friends is that we really don't have access to the total picture.

*O God, help me to recognize that my teen is making value-based decisions every day about which friends to get closer to and which ones he needs to move away from. Please stay with him as he travels this path. Watch over him, Lord. Keep him close to your heart.*

She found out that one of her best friends didn't invite her to a party. She was crushed! And the way she found out was so cruel. Someone sent her an e-mail saying she wasn't invited because boys were going to be there, and they didn't think she could "handle" it.

Girls can be especially cruel as the social order develops during the middle school years. We need to give our daughters tools to defend themselves. They need to learn how to deal with peer bullying and cliques.

*Help her, Holy Spirit, to deal with this disappointment and to believe in and defend her dignity. Guide us toward resources that will help her define the kind of person she wants to be.*

Teenage boys! They are so loud and in your face and are so just *there*. Music blaring. Radio blasting. Shouting. Yelling. They take up such physical space in a room. Look at me! Everything's exaggerated.

Sometimes my sister wishes she had teenage girls. They seem quieter. She thinks she could relate to them better; they could share more things. She tells me there's so much she doesn't understand about teenage boys.

*O God, help all mothers to understand their sons. Let us use this opportunity to grow and stretch into more whole and complete persons. Our sons need to know that women can be strong, intelligent, and hard working. Show all of us the ways in which our sons and we are exactly the same.*

Teenage girls! They laugh so loud in your face and are so just *there*. Music blaring. Radio blasting. Crying. Yelling. They take up so much emotional space. Listen to me! Everything's exaggerated.

Sometimes my brother wishes he had teenage boys. He thinks he could relate to them better, they could share more things. He says, "There's so much I don't understand about teenage girls."

*O God, help all fathers everywhere to understand and find ways to connect to their daughters. Our girls need to know that men can be tender and kind, sensitive and loving. Show these fathers all the ways in which our daughters and they are exactly the same.*

"A teenaged girl decided right before entering college that she was not meant to go to college and never had been. She was sure that if she took four months off to perfect her study habits and separate more gradually from her boyfriend, she might be able to face it—for surely, she thought, no eighteen-year-old on the face of the planet was as messed up as she is. Her parents said, 'Ah, we know this place.'

"But when the crucial moment came, the young woman packed up and headed for college as planned. When she moved into her dorm, she called her mother and said, "I think I'm going to like it here. Her mother said, 'Ah, I know this place.'

"In the morning she called her father crying, saying she was too lonely to bear it. Her father said, 'Ah, I know this place.'

"Change does not come in neat packages. It never has and it never will. Ah, we know this place."

*A story from John Morgan's* Awakening the Soul

*O Mary, you watched your child Jesus as he set off by himself out into the world. Help my child as she struggles to separate from me. Help me to remember:* I know this place.

We have packed the car, maps in hand, catalogues scattered on the floor by our feet. Our college tour! We circle the country, or at least it feels that way, rushing from campus to campus. Soon everything is a blur; every college begins to look like the last one. We're exhausted!

So much anxiety and stress. Will he pick the college that's right for him? Will they want him?

We need to keep everything in perspective during this time. Many schools will be a good match for our teen. We have to trust that God has a plan for all of our children.

*Wise God, help us to be patient and discerning as we try to sift through this enormous amount of information. Help us to know that you are watching over us as we travel this unknown and exciting path.*

He's discovered a way to make us laugh. When we are in the throes of battle, or when things are getting tense, he has learned how to use humor to lighten things up. What a gift! What a relief! We don't have to take ourselves so seriously anymore—at least not all the time.

*Thank you, God, for giving us the grace to appreciate our teen's gift of humor in the midst of turmoil. Let our teen's sense of comedic timing serve him well in the years to come.*

She doesn't want to go to the movies with us or to be seen with us *anywhere* in public. A new mandate, almost overnight. What's so wrong with us? How do we not take this personally?

Most teens feel embarrassed by their parents—if that's any consolation for the hurt and rejection we can't help but feel. It's during times like this that we must picture our teens as their future selves. Can you imagine any respectable thirty-year-old insisting that her elderly father walk ten steps behind her at the mall?!

*God, please remind me during the times that I feel unwanted that "this too shall pass."*

I laugh, extra loud, at the commercials that show parents gleefully shopping for school supplies. My children groan. They know it's almost time to go back to school.

There's a different kind of energy in the house: anxious, excited, and worried. We're all a bit on edge.

*Dear God, help us as we transition toward summer's end. Bless my children with a school year that's full of success and positive learning experiences.*

"We do have seasons when we enjoy the delight and the adventure of life's travels, when we savor the taste of recovered hope and relish the vistas of new truths."

*Joyce Rupp*

September beckons: new pencils, books, school clothes. But the school year brings more than just learning. What new people will enter our lives this year, bringing fresh perspectives and new ideas?

*O God, bless us as we journey into this new season. Keep our minds and hearts open to all that awaits us. Help us anticipate these changes with joy.*

# September

## ***September 1***

We're going over the photographs we took last week of the colleges we visited. Somehow, we need to make a decision about where he's going to apply in the next few months. He's still needs to fill out applications, write essays, go on interviews, and, in the midst of it all, keep up with his academic schedule and all the other things he has to do.

*Wise and tender God, help my son to stay focused on his goals. Give him the time and the energy to accomplish all of his objectives. Guide him in this important decision.*

My son is smaller than most of the other kids his age, and he's nervous about starting high school. It's a big school—he could get lost there! We've heard rumors about some of the older kids pushing around the younger ones, directing them to the wrong classroom, or making fun of them on the bus.

As in most things, the unknown can sometimes seem unmanageable and scary. Most teens find the adjustment to high school a relatively easy one, and they enjoy the increased independence coupled with more responsibilities. But some have a tough time socially, especially that first year. These days, almost all high schools have policies and procedures in place to make the transition as smooth as possible. It helps to encourage our children to go to visit the new school beforehand as much as possible, to become familiar with the physical surroundings so it's not as intimidating. We can also remind our teens of the other transitions they have successfully mastered in the past.

*Please God, watch over my teen as he begins this next adventure. Help him see that when he puts his faith in you, everything works out.*

Tomorrow is my sister's birthday. I am sad that we cannot be together to share the day, because she lives too far away. I remember when we lived close enough, we could celebrate together, and I could watch her blow out the candles. My daughter saw me, teary-eyed with the memory, and I shared my feelings with her so that she could realize a little better how blessed—and limited—is this time we have together as *this* family.

*O God, help me to share my sadness with my teens so they will know about life's bittersweet moments. They need a glimpse of the future occasionally so that they will cherish the present and remember to honor the past.*

It's been hard for them to get up early after becoming used to sleeping late. And things have been so chaotic trying to get to the bus stop on time, finding classes, and forgetting homework or lunches or papers that need to be signed. It seems as if we've suddenly blasted into a school year and it's left us yearning for those slow-paced days of summer.

*O God, help us to adjust to this new and hectic schedule. Remind us to allow ourselves more time than we think we need, so that we can stay on track with all there is to do.*

## *September 5*

Our son announced that, unlike all of his friends, he's not going to college next year. He's decided to put it off for at least a year...or maybe he'll never go. We are disappointed, and we've spent so much time trying to persuade him otherwise, pointing out the ramifications of his decision, but he's adamant. He says he isn't sure what career path he wants to pursue. We have no choice; we have to try to understand. Yet, when we tell other parents, they look at us as if we've failed him somehow. As difficult as this is, we need to be able to tolerate his ambivalence, while at the same time expect him to take responsibility for his life.

Many roads can lead to the same destination—hopefully, to our child's happiness. When our teens choose a different road, it can be hard on them, but it can be hard on us, too, especially when others don't understand. We need to help our teens to formulate a plan that is right for them, which includes a realistic budget and steps toward their future. Perhaps they would join the military, go to a trade school, or intern in a career area they may want to pursue.

*O God, show me how to support my young adult in making the decisions that are right for* him, *even when his road looks completely different from his friends' or what I envisioned for him.*

My fourteen-year-old daughter told me that she thinks she has romantic feelings toward another girl! I was astonished, flabbergasted, angry, worried, hurt. So many emotions swirl around me, I don't know where to turn. Is this just a phase? Is it my fault? How will we ever deal with this?

We need to talk openly with our teens so we can learn and understand more about what they are experiencing, and encouraging them to remain chaste, regardless of their feelings. Many young teens go through a period of confusion about their sexuality, and it has nothing to do with what we did or didn't do as parents. Our teens may be lost and anxious and not know where to turn. As hard as it may seem, we need to be there for them and listen to them through this incredibly difficult time.

*God of mercy, hear my cry. I am feeling lost and alone and unsure. Please help our family. Help us to find ways to support each other. Help me to remember most of all that my teen needs my unyielding love. Help my child to deepen her faith in you, our God, and bring her ever closer to your glory.*

My daughter has been on the bench. She's tried her hardest, but the coach doesn't give her a chance. He yells at her when she makes mistakes and puts her down in front of everyone. She's thinking about quitting the team. She's not enjoying the sport anymore. We think she should stick with her commitment—but she's so frustrated and tearful after every game. Is there ever a time when quitting is okay?

Sometimes leaving a situation can be an invaluable lesson for the future. Would we want our children to stay in an unhealthy work situation or abusive relationship? It's important to give people feedback, letting them know that we need to be treated with decency. If they can't or won't respond appropriately, then it may be time to walk away.

*Dear God, help our teen to make a decision that will maintain her sense of self-worth and dignity.*

Our son often says, "I'm no good. I'll never get it." He has so little confidence. It's as if he's treading water just trying to keep up with things. Still, there are other times when he surprises us and seems to sail right through.

We all need encouragement and to have someone who believes in us. We all need someone who will say, "I love you. I trust you. I know it's hard, but you can do this. I have faith in you. I believe in you."

*Loving God, please help me to be a voice of encouragement for my teen, as you are always that voice for me in my life.*

### *September 9*

My daughter went to her first high school dance tonight. I've heard from other parents that some of the kids in her grade are already using drugs and alcohol. I'm so afraid for her innocence. She is trustworthy, but naive. How can I protect her from those dangerous kids?

Teens will usually gravitate toward peers who share their values. No one can force another person to use drugs if he or she doesn't want to. Still, it is wise to talk with our teens about ways they can protect themselves when they find themselves in uncomfortable situations. We may let them know that they can *always* call us, using a code word perhaps, if they need to leave somewhere in a hurry—with no questions asked!

*Holy Spirit, let me know that you are with my teen always, like a shining light guiding her toward safe decisions and protecting her from harm.*

"Worry is the price you pay in advance for most of the things in life that will never happen."

*Mark Twain*

But what about when the worst thing *does* happen? How do we reassure our children when images of tragedy from nearby and far away confront them every day? How can we give them messages about hope when all around them the world seems filled with horrific events?

*Jesus, Prince of Peace, remind us that you are with us always. Everything we do in life carries a certain element of risk, but* to live life fully *is one of life's greatest blessings. You have taught us this. Please keep us safe in all we do, and keep our loved ones close to your heart.*

"Help, O Lord, for there is no longer anyone who is godly;
the faithful have disappeared from humankind."

*Psalm 12:1*

Sometimes the world around us seems so full of sadness. Our hearts break for the misery of others, and we are afraid of all the evil in the world.

Good and evil have always existed side by side. Our teens need the tools to help them cope with unspeakable loss, and ways to feel like they are helping when they see others in utter pain. We can encourage our teens to seek out ways to help through volunteering or fundraising for various causes. We can tell our teens that it helps to turn to God when the world seems lost. Jesus has already overcome evil, and we can ask him to comfort those in pain. And if we allow him, God will always help us with our fears.

*Our Father, who art in Heaven, hallowed be thy name. Thy kingdom come, thy will be done on earth as it is in heaven. Give us this day our daily bread and deliver us from evil...for thine is the kingdom, and the power and the glory, forever and ever. Amen.*

"That's when I began to see despair for what it is: a wake-up call to connect. What brings me out of despair every time is attending to the living, breathing world right in front of me."

*Kimberly Ridley*

When I'm feeling burdened by the sadness of the world, how do I deal with it? How do I model for my teen what to do with despair?

*O God, we are sometimes surrounded by despair in this world. Let me be a listening ear for those who need to be heard. Let me be a loving heart for those who need to be comforted. Let me be a compassionate voice for those who need to hear your soothing words.*

My daughter had never been in a championship tennis match before, and frankly, she's never been a particularly good player. But something happened yesterday. She was on fire! Her backhand was relentless and she was just burning up the court. And when the match was over, she had won. It was amazing!

Sometimes we can call upon an inner strength that we didn't even know existed. We soar above expectations and come through for others and ourselves. It's as if God is especially with us at those times, watching and whispering, "Yes, yes, you can do this. All things are possible through me."

*Help my teen, O God, to draw upon your gift of inner strength daily. Guide her to be the best that she can be.*

My husband has decided to read all of the books our daughter has to read for her English class this year. He wants to have something to share with her. They've created their own "book club." Every month or so, they go out to lunch and "talk books." She feels proud and important as she shares with him insights from her class.

When was the last time I tried to learn something new? Learning together—whether it's a new sport, language, or musical instrument—can be a wonderful way of growing and connecting with our teens. They get to see us in situations where we feel awkward and unsure. We get to spend precious time with them. When was the last time I let my teen teach me something?

*Dear Jesus, help me to continue to be open to the process of learning and growing. Let us be aware of the new things we can learn and share as a family–as your family.*

Our son's friends are allowed to stay out past midnight on the weekends; but we have set his curfew for 11:00 P.M. We are convinced that nothing good is happening in this town after midnight! Every time he comes home early, he reminds us that *everyone* gets to stay out later than he does.

We are *not* everyone else. We are *our* family. We must believe in our ability to parent the best we can, while continuing to remain open to negotiation as the situation evolves and changes.

*O God, help us to stand strong behind our convictions. Through you, we can stay true to what is right for our family.*

Our son has lied to us again. It's becoming a chronic problem. We've had numerous issues with him for years, but now that he's a teenager, he's out of control. We're ready to give in and send him to his grandparents' house, where he says he'd rather live anyway. But we feel like such failures.

Teen dysfunction can be incredibly stressful, especially when a teen expresses a strong desire to live somewhere else. Sometimes families can benefit from a separation, and teens may learn that they bring their problems with them wherever they go. This takes coordination and trust in a power greater than ourselves. Often, troubled teens eventually return to their family better able to appreciate our love for them—though there is no guarantee.

*God, our Father, please hear our prayer. Reassure us that we have all done the best we could, in a difficult situation. Help us be open to recognize where we could do better. Please guide us in this important decision. Show us how to deal with this crisis in a way that respects the integrity of everyone involved.*

I sit at the kitchen window watching a squirrel. He's frantically racing up and down a tree, burying his nuts in the backyard. Up and down, back and forth, over and over again. It's only September, I want to tell him. Slow down, little friend. What's the rush?

What am I doing frantically? Where am I racing to in my life? When do I need to slow down? Am I driving, eating, working, shopping, and *living* too fast?

*Holy Mary, woman blessed in the art of patient waiting, please help me to recognize that I don't always have to live life at a frenetic pace. Show me how to slow down and enjoy the gifts our heavenly Father has given me.*

Her hair is in dreadlocks. He wants to wear black all the time *and* metal studded belts and bracelets! It's embarrassing to be seen with them! They're carving out a niche for themselves in the world that seems so strange and different.

The way our teens choose to dress is another way of differentiating themselves and separating from us. We need to remind them, however, that *how* they present themselves communicates something of *who* they are to the world. Getting upset or overreacting is not the best way to handle the situation. Allowing them to wear certain clothes at home or on weekends, and others for school and church can be a compromise. We can negotiate with them about ways they can show their uniqueness, but at the same time, they can learn to be flexible in how and where they express that part of themselves.

*O God, you made us all uniquely different–even down to our fingerprints! What a complex and marvelous design is the human person. Help me see my teen's uniqueness in his way of expressing himself. Help us to find compromises that preserve the moral code of our family and allow him to present his best to the world.*

I feel as if we are endlessly transporting our son to his many social obligations, school, and sports-related functions. But what about our social life? He's sixteen. He's old enough to be left alone at home, so why should we worry about going out every Friday night? Don't we deserve a social life, too?

It's important to be emotionally and physically "there" for our children when they reach their teenage years. Empty houses and teenagers aren't a good mix. It's when they're coming down this last "home stretch" that they need us most of all. Besides, our teens can't do their job of separating from us if we're not around to separate *from.* Certainly it's important for us to nourish our adult relationships, and it is okay to go out once in while, but not so regularly that *our* social lives take precedence and our teens feel too often alone and neglected.

*Help us, O God, to put our need for a social life temporarily on hold and help us to remember that this too shall pass. Too soon, we will have more than enough free time on our hands.*

I saw an old friend at the high school's open house. Our eyes connected, we shared a few laughs, and then we both apologized for letting so much time lapse since we saw each other last. We promised to get together soon, but part of me wondered if that will really happen.

What's stopping me from making time for this good friend? Have I let my busy schedule prevent me from getting together with her? Or have I just been too lazy?

*Jesus, help me to say "yes" more often to the people and experiences that nourish me spiritually, for this is what will bring me closer to you.*

She's happy, just plain happy. She sings to herself when she's walking through a room. She bounces, her eyes glisten, and her smile radiates from the inside. She giggles and laughs, and sometimes she even gives us a hug.

Perfect grades or being the star of the team does not really matter. What college she gets into, or what job she gets eventually, or whether or not she marries, or has money, or...or...these things don't really matter either. At present, *nothing* matters as much as this one thing: she's *happy* with her life.

*Dear God, thank you for the gift of our happy teen.*

My son has been sick for over a month. He's tired and can't seem to hold food down. He's missed the entire first month of school. The doctors don't know what's wrong with him. All the tests have come back negative. We've brought him to specialists, but still, there is so much that they don't know. He may have to be hospitalized if things don't change soon. I'm so scared.

We feel powerless when our children are sick. We want so much to take their pain away. We can't help but think back to easier times and wonder why we ever worried over comparatively trivial things.

*God of Compassion, hear my cry. My child is sick and my prayers are constant. Please don't abandon us. Please heal my son.*

He's entering a leadership program next summer with a special group from our high school. We couldn't be more proud. What an opportunity! What an adventure! I rushed to the phone and called everyone I know to tell them the news, and, later, when I went out, I found myself casually slipping the good news into every conversation.

It can be tempting sometimes, but we have to remember not to brag about our child's accomplishments. Rather, we can share with those who seem truly interested in how our teen is doing. Another family may be experiencing difficulties, and hearing of our good fortune may be painful.

*Thank you, O God, for the gift of success for our teen. Help him to use his leadership abilities to do positive things, bringing your message of love and good will toward all.*

My friend's daughter has struggled with the effects of Spinal Bifida all her life. She walks with a limp and because of medical procedures has missed so much time from school that she's only now graduating, at nineteen. She is so brave. Sometimes my heart just breaks to see all she has endured, and I'm so afraid for her, and for my friend—for what's to come.

When I talk to my friend about my worries, she tells me that she feels blessed to have had her daughter in her life. She says she already did her mourning, long ago, and feels confident that her faith will help her get through whatever the future may bring.

*Thank you, God, for the blessing of all the "special" children in our lives. Please give them the courage to live in the world where they must face so many challenges. Please guide others to treat them with compassion and understanding. Watch over these families with love, until the time comes when all of your children return home to you.*

My neighbor has always known that the day would come when her adopted daughter might want to find her birth mother. Still, she wasn't prepared for how much it would hurt! She worries about how this might complicate her daughter's life. The girl is only eighteen. Her daughter says she's just curious, and that she loves them as her parents. Then why does she have to find her birth mother? Or more importantly, why *now*?

All teens struggle with issues of identity. "Who am I?" and "Who do I want to become?" are prevalent themes as they begin to prepare themselves for adulthood. These issues can be especially difficult for an adopted child. If we can appreciate an adopted child's struggle, and feel secure in our role as adoptive parents, then it's probably okay to help them to proceed in their search—slowly! If there are signs that the child or birth parent isn't handling it well emotionally, then we may need to take a few steps back; and possibly obtain some professional guidance with how to proceed.

*O God, please guide my neighbor's daughter as she searches for her biological roots. Help her parents to stay open to all that this search may hold for her. Please continue to protect their daughter from areas that may be too difficult for her to manage right now.*

As a therapist, during sessions when parents complain about their difficult teens, I will sometimes choose to share a story about how one of my children has misbehaved in the past. This is to let my patients know that even we "experts" have a rough time with our own kids. As a young therapist, I was wary about sharing personal revelations, thinking I might lose some of my credibility. But lately I've found that parents often breathe a sigh of relief when I do share personal experiences. It's as if they suddenly understand that we're all in this together. We've *all* experienced the same thing. Suddenly we're laughing and learning from one another.

There is much solace in understanding that along with joy, we *all* have moments of doubt, frustration, fear, remorse, and sadness—it's all part of raising teenagers.

*Dear God, help me to share my awkward places of parenting with my community of parents. Help me not to judge when someone takes the risk of sharing with me. We can learn from each other. We don't need to feel alone. When we open our hearts to others, we open our hearts to you, our God.*

When my mother comes to visit and asks my teen to do something, he does it willingly, without a complaint! She smiles at me smugly when this happens. It gets me so mad! She says, "If you'd only ask him nicely, he'd do anything you want."

Some teens develop close bonds with their grandparents. It can be easier for them to relate to the older generation, without the struggle of separation getting in the way. At times, those relationships can become problematic if we allow them to interfere with our authority as parents. It may sometimes be necessary to say gently to our in-laws or parents, "I need to handle this on my own," or, "Your thoughts on this are not helpful right now," when we sense a relative might be overstepping boundaries.

*Patient God, help me be patient with the older adults in my life who try to offer me suggestions on how to deal with my teen. Let me not shut out everything they have to say, as there may be some kernels of wisdom in their true desire to help.*

Our daughter is failing two classes. At this rate, we're wondering if she'll be able to graduate. We're not sure what to do. If we suggest anything to her, or remind her (as we do constantly) of what she needs to do, she just tells us to "lay off," and talks about how she'll be out on her own soon enough.

As parents, we can fall into the nasty habit of nagging underachievers. Sometimes the best approach is simply to ask our teens, "What is your plan?" Asking them step-by-step what they expect to happen can give them the skills they need to solve their problems.

It can also help if we step back from the situation long enough to say, "Let us know if you need us. Unless we hear from you, we trust that you can take care of this." Teens seldom want to fail, but they do need to feel that *they* are making the decision to succeed.

*God, our Father, you gave us the gift of free will. Help us to step back and let our teen make the decision to fail or succeed. Help her be open to accepting our help–if or when she needs it. She will learn much in the process if she knows it is truly her decision alone to make.*

All my friends told me that this year would be different, that maturity would finally kick in, and he would begin to take charge of his life. But what a change! Is this the same kid who once had to be dragged out of bed every morning to catch the bus? He's busy all the time now—responsible, kind, and helpful. Whew! Have we really crossed a new threshold?

Whether we believe it or not *everything* will come together for most of our kids. Of course, there will still be trials and tribulations. Certainly, things will continue to change, but the transition from adolescence to adulthood is one of the most exciting and rewarding phases of parenting and the sweetness of the reward is sometimes greater if we've experienced a few bumps along the way.

*Thank you, sweet God, for the gift of our emerging young adult. I am so grateful that we've almost made it through this transition.*

The coach expects them to be at practice every day for three hours, even if they have a test the next day or another commitment, such as church or music lessons. If they miss a practice, they won't play the next game—no matter what. Other school activities involve almost the same level of commitment. When I talk to other parents, they simply shrug their shoulders and go along with these impossible expectations, even though they secretly admit it's too much and worry about their teen becoming overstressed or exhausted.

As parents, we need to speak out when society begins to dictate what is right for our children.

*Help us, O God, to prioritize what is truly important. Let us begin to have the conversation with other parents about the price our teens might pay for trying to do or have it all.*

# October

She came home from school in tears. Her teacher caught her cheating on a homework assignment and gave her (and the friend she copied from) a zero. My daughter said it wasn't as if she were cheating on a test; it was *only* homework. She had meant to do the assignment the day before, but she "forgot." She said she was just "cutting a few corners."

Unfortunately, cheating is so common in our high schools, and many of our teens don't even realize that they're doing it. Some of them rationalize that it's the only way to stay on top of things—especially if they aren't caught. Sadly, it only cheapens their work and the work of others.

How am I modeling integrity for my teens? Are there places in my life where I "cut corners" by not being truly honest?

*Dear God, help us to explore the values of integrity and honor, and to teach our children the importance of representing ourselves honestly in everything we do. Remind us that when we are honest, we honor your gifts, O Lord.*

I'm having trouble falling asleep at night. There is so much going on in my life. My mind keeps playing my "to-do" list over and over, trying to remember it all, wondering how I will ever manage to get everything done... I toss and turn. When I arise not fully rested, I laugh to myself as I mentally add: "not getting enough sleep" onto my list of things to worry about.

Taking a long time to fall asleep, early morning waking, and rising from bed not feeling rested can be attributed to having too much stress—or they can be early warning signs of depression. It's just as important to pay attention to our own mental health as the mental health of our teens. If sleep disturbances last for more than two weeks, and are accompanied by feelings of sadness or anxiety, it may be time to consult a health professional.

*O God, help me to remember to ask you to be with me during times of sleeplessness and anxiety. It feels so good to imagine you whispering to me: "Don't worry, now. You will have more than enough time to do all that you truly need to do. Let go, and I will take care of the rest."*

## *October 3*

I've had to ground my son again—this time for a month. We've taken away every possible privilege. But still nothing changes. No matter what we say, we can't seem to get through to him.

Perhaps the most effective and memorable consequences for our children are the ones that result naturally from their actions. With teens, this sometimes requires a bit more thought and creativity. Rather than grounding them for life or restricting all privileges, we must somehow tie the consequence to the action. If a chore is forgotten, maybe we can "forget" to do something for him or her? If he or she is leaving trash in our car, maybe can we leave trash in his or her room?

*O God, show me how and when to act unpredictably toward my teen to bring home a lesson. Remind me that it is my job as his parent to teach him responsible behavior. Words alone are not always as effective as actions. Help me not to overreact as I struggle to find a balance and keep things in perspective.*

This morning at church, we had a blessing for the animals in honor of St. Francis. We brought our dog. There were lots of dogs there, a few cats, a guinea pig, a rabbit, a hermit crab, a few mice, and a snake. My teenager thought it was kind of a silly idea, and I could see his point. But then the priest talked about how our pet's devotion to us was a way of experiencing God's unconditional love. All of a sudden, my son looked at our dog and smiled.

*Help us, dear Lord, to protect the animals that you entrust to our care. In their wordless communication, in devotion, and in selflessness, they truly can help us remember your unconditional love.*

Our daughter's cat, Fluffy, spends hours on her bed. She used to dress him up when she was a little girl. Now the cat holds all her tears. She doesn't have to be "cool" around the cat. She doesn't have to worry about what she looks like or what she wears. Fluffy is there to love and to be loved. It's as simple and as wonderful as that.

As our teens become more mature, it can be more difficult for them to give us a hug or let us hold them when they are feeling sad. Family pets can fill a valuable need for the expression of love, touch, and compassion in the life of our teen.

*Thank you, dear God, for the gift of our family pet in my teen's life.*

I drove past a rather beaten-down part of the city today. I tried to imagine the reality of those who live there. What struggles they must deal with every day? How do those teenagers deal with the difficulties that poverty, drugs, and crime bring to their doorstep? There's so much that needs to be done! I don't want to think about it—it's too overwhelming. What could I possibly do to make a difference?

Small steps. Small, one-at-a-time, steps. If everyone did just one small thing, the world would change drastically for the better—overnight. When was the last time I brought food to the local food bank, volunteered to tutor a child, or helped out at a soup kitchen? When was the last time my teens volunteered? These are things we can do together with our teens to help others in need.

*God of compassion, when we find ourselves stuck in the same place, too busy to help, too tired to care, nudge us toward your service. We need to hear your voice saying to our hearts: "You can do this one small thing. Through me you can do this one small thing...and then another."*

My brother's adopted daughter is one of a few minority children at her high school. They moved into this school system last year, anticipating some prejudice, but, luckily, until now there hadn't been much. Unfortunately, the other day she overheard a group of girls in the hallway making derogatory comments—about her! A teacher spotted them, scolded the girls, and forced them to apologize. Still, his daughter was devastated. Now my brother is wondering if they made the right decision to move here.

Prejudice wears an ugly face. Have I ever felt the sting of rejection based on how I looked, dressed, or worshiped? Have I ever found myself treating people differently because they seem different from me?

*Dear God, help our teens stay strong in the face of unfairness and oppression. Help them reach out to others who are different in an effort to understand them.*

I didn't grow up in a demonstrative family. We never hugged or touched much, and I never remember my parents saying, "I love you." Now that my son is growing up, it's harder than ever to express physical affection toward him. I guess since I'm his mother, he feels he needs to push me away even further.

Our teens still need physical contact from us, but in ways that respect their changing boundaries. They need to see the love in our eyes when we look at them, to hear the love in our voices when we talk to them, and to feel the love in our arms when we tell them that we simply *must* have a hug.

*Heavenly Father, help me to express the depth of my love for my teen, even when it sometimes feels awkward and uncomfortable for either of us. Guide me to recognize how you express the depth of your love for me, in all of your blessings.*

Every time I see this certain man, it makes my blood boil. He coaches just about every sport in town, and all he cares about is winning. Everyone knows he's unfair. He keeps his best team members playing longer than they should, and doesn't give everyone on the team a chance to play. Nobody likes him, and now my son has him for a coach!

Loving our neighbor is hard. It is *so* hard, especially when we believe that our neighbor is not worthy of it, or when we think our children could be hurt.

How can I learn from this experience? Can I find the gift that might be hidden in this situation? Could this experience be a gift of learning about tolerance, or standing up for what's right for my child in a way that respects everyone involved?

*O Jesus, help me, because hate threatens to invade my heart. Open my eyes to your face in this stranger's face. Help me to learn about your compassionate love when loving my neighbor feels so very hard.*

Shalom—a Jewish greeting. A hope that the person you are greeting is in a right relationship with God and other human beings. Peace, integrity, wholeness: these are the wishes implied.

How do I greet others? Am I so focused on everything I have to do that I forget to notice others? Do I notice my neighbors who are struggling with the same issues as I am?

*God, show me how to greet others in the spirit of kindness. Help me to remember to slow down when I am hurrying. I need to notice: Your face in their faces. Your eyes in their eyes. Your breath. Your love. You.*

Two teens were arrested last week for bringing weapons into our local high school. They didn't hurt anyone, but what if they had? There's so much violence in the world—sometimes I feel so helpless and vulnerable. Aren't my children safe anywhere?

Teenagers can reflect the worst parts of society, and it is somehow more shocking to us because they are still children. We can do something about the violence in our communities, and one person *can* make a difference. How? By volunteering at a crisis center, mentoring a disadvantaged teen, or encouraging our parent-teacher organization to support programs on anti-bullying. Our children need to know that they can also help. Every day they can make choices to be role models for others: to defend the weak, to be kind, to be a banner of peace for their school community.

*Peaceful God, guide us toward becoming part of the solution to violence in our society. Show us where we can best be of service to our community.*

Recently, in a nearby town, a young girl was drugged and raped in the woods behind the high school. It makes me want to scream that this kind of thing can happen! It has destroyed this girl's life—and now it affects ours as well. My daughter is afraid to go to school, and who can blame her?

Teens can be traumatized when something terrible happens so close to home. It's natural for them to want to stay at home, where they feel more safe and secure. It's important to encourage them to face their fears, armed with confidence and a strong faith.

*Holy Spirit, help us through this awful experience. Give us the courage to face our fears. Help us to heal from this tragedy and to know that through you we are blessed and capable of doing things we could never do alone.*

I was riding on a bus with a group of my son's teammates. I couldn't believe the profane language they were using right in front of me! When I was a kid, I would never have talked like that in front of an adult.

Kids in a group will sometimes do things that they would never do if they were alone. It takes courage to say something to a group of teens without feeling anxious and outnumbered. Most of the time, teens will react positively and learn from the experience.

*O God, help me to know that your words spoken through me can make a difference. Give me the courage to know what words to say and how and when to say them.*

The referee made a call that clearly disappointed my daughter. She stomped off the field and then cursed loud enough for him to hear. He then ejected her from the game. I wanted to say something about the call being unfair, but something stopped me. I realized that maybe the referee was right.

My teen needs to learn how to handle life's disappointments more maturely. Have I somehow not paid enough attention to this unsportsmanlike behavior? It's never too late to help our teens learn how to become better people. This is our job as parents.

*Help me, O God, to step back sometimes from the role of "protector" and allow my teen to become a mature person. Help her recognize that her actions speak louder than words, that her words speak volumes about her character. Please help her to be a better person.*

It seems it happens this way every year. Almost overnight, all the leaves have turned colors and the trees are like glorious tents of crimson high above our heads. How I love it when they reach their peak, but it makes me a little sad too. A few weeks from now the wind and weather will knock them down, brown, and ugly beneath our feet.

Sometimes it feels as though all the good things we've put into our teen have been forgotten, that they've fallen away, gone to waste, never to return.

Those good things are still there; it's just that they've been blown around in the wild wind—temporarily.

*Help me notice, O God, when those good things emerge in my teen. When I notice the good, it will encourage more of the same.*

My son was invited to a Bat Mitzvah; a new experience for him. He didn't have a suit jacket, so we went shopping. I noticed he was quiet and suddenly in a bad mood at the store. Finally, the day arrived. He looked very handsome in his new suit jacket and tie, but there was that bad mood again. What was this all about? *"I'm worried,"* he said. *"I've never been to a Bat Mitzvah before. What if I don't know what to do?"*

I told him not to worry, that there would be dancing at the party and lots of good food. His job was to have fun and eat. And for some reason I felt compelled to remind him: don't forget to dance.

When he came home, he was all smiles, saying he had a great time and bragging that he and another boy were the first ones to dance. Later he got a card from the girl saying, "Thank you for coming to my Bat Mitzvah. Thank you for dancing. You made the party great."

*Thank you, generous God, for inspiring me with the right words to say at the right time and allowing my teen to hear them.*

My daughter has been procrastinating about sending out her college applications. She tells me she'll get it done, not to worry, that it's *her* responsibility, but a part of me wants to make sure. If she can't take care of this, how will she ever be ready to go out into the world?

As our teens prepare to launch out on their own, a part of us wants to hold on tighter than ever before. We want to make sure that they have everything taken care of—before it's too late. Personality flaws and other unresolved issues become more glaring as their childhood comes to its end.

Instead of thinking we have to "fix" them before it's too late, we need to recognize that their adulthood journey has only just begun. They will have a whole lifetime to get it right.

*Loving God, help my teen take responsibility for her life. I am afraid that she isn't ready for all the world's challenges. Guide her as she makes decisions. Help me to step aside when it's time, but please be there to catch her if she falls.*

She spends hours showering, changing outfits, and studying her reflection in the mirror. I keep trying to tell her that what's on the *inside* matters, but she gets so frustrated with me and tells me that I just don't understand.

Teens, especially young teens, can suddenly become focused on appearance. It's all part of their changing body image. While I want her to value what's inside, I need to remember that it's natural for her to be concerned about the outside, too. With the onset of puberty, her body is changing in so many dramatic ways!

*Mary, help me to be a voice of understanding. Help me talk to my teen about her appearance in ways that are supportive, yet lend perspective to this time of her life. Let me be a voice of reassurance and unconditional love, as you are that voice to me.*

"I have found that the best way to give advice to your children is to find out what they want and then advise them to do it."

*Harry S. Truman*

Teens have an infuriating way of disregarding our advice; at least it often appears that way. They want and need to discover things for themselves, and they don't want anyone—much less a middle-aged parent—telling them what to do! A major task of adolescence is developing the ability to make wise and independent decisions, even if it means that some of their decisions will appear foolish.

When we think they are attempting to do something that might be a bit off base, it can help if we calmly say, "Tell me what you think the consequences of this decision might be."

*Dear Lord, please stop me when I am about to give unsolicited advice, and allow my teen to develop her sense of how to make good decisions.*

My daughter is stressed out. She is taking three honors courses, is very involved in theater, and participates in two clubs at school. She's snapping at us and weepy, but she refuses to even consider giving up any of her activities.

As parents, we need to intervene when our teens appear to be overloaded. They may not have the ability to discern what is most important when they are in the midst of so much activity. We can help them by suggesting exercise or meditation and daily prayer to help keep them rested and their stress level low. However, there just isn't time to "do it all," and we need to let them know that it's okay to make selective choices about how to spend their time.

*O God, help my teen to seek solitude and spiritual centering in her life. Show her that time spent in daily prayer can be restorative and a source of great peace and strength.*

"The teenage years are like passing through a long tunnel. If your kid is okay before they go in, they should be okay on the way out. But I'm not exactly sure what happens while they're in there."

*Anonymous*

When do I feel doubt about how my teen will turn out? What do I need to do to replace that doubt with confidence? Can I let go of trying to control the outcome, while, at the same time, allowing myself to enter into and be changed by the process of raising a teenager?

*O God of light, help me on this journey. There are times when I am so anxious and worried about what will happen to my teen. Hold my hand and walk with my teen and me through this dark tunnel toward the light of my teen's emerging adulthood.*

Whenever my daughter is tired, or hungry, or sick with a minor cold, she whines and complains, acting badly toward those around her. Everything is such a dramatic ordeal. I want to shout, "Get over it! Toughen up!" And sometimes I do.

How our children act when they are feeling weak or vulnerable can evoke powerful feelings in us, often stemming from how our parents treated weakness in our own childhood. Who took care of me when I was sick? Was I expected to minimize my pain? Or did I get to stay at home, pampered, until I was feeling better?

We all need sympathy when we aren't feeling well, but many of us don't know how to express our needs in a way that will help us receive loving care.

*O God, help me to take care of my teen when she is sick, while placing limits on her demanding tone. Remind me that no matter how I was treated when I was a child, I can now choose how I want to treat my teens–and that I can ask for care from them when I need it, too.*

**Get over it!** 

Lately my oldest daughter has been so mean to her younger sister. "She's so annoying!" the eldest cries, as she banishes her from the room, or flatly ignores the younger one's pleas for attention.

Straddling a tightrope between childhood and adulthood, teenagers are trying to separate from anything that seems childish. Privacy becomes more important, as do boundary issues around friends, music, and clothing. New teens especially have a tendency to lash out at reminders of their younger selves, including, unfortunately, younger siblings.

I may need to explore with my teen why her sister has "suddenly" become so frustrating. I can teach my younger child how to ask for attention in more positive ways. It can help to share with them what I observe about the dynamic between them, showing them how to renegotiate their changing relationship.

*Help me, dear God, to give my teens the relationship tools that they will carry into their adulthood, so that they can be a source of loving support for one another for years to come. This is your true and loving desire for them, and for all of us.*

A neighbor shared with me the differences between his two girls. He said one daughter is easy, like a shaft of sunlight warming you on an autumn day. "And the other?" I asked. He hesitated, then said, "Well, have you ever gotten a pebble stuck in your shoe?"

How can two children raised in the same family be so different? How can one know exactly how to please us and do it most of the time, and another be a constant struggle, irritating, non-compliant, "rubbing us the wrong way"?

Children have different temperaments, and they are not always a good match with our personality. But the child who gives us the most grief also has the capacity to give us the greatest gift: the opportunity to stretch ourselves spiritually.

*Mother of God, help me to recognize the gifts my "difficult" teen holds for me. Help me parent in a way that respects and embraces our differences–and the ways in which we are exactly the same!*

The days are becoming shorter now. I drive to work and come home in darkness. How I dread this time of year, everything dying, cold, and without promise. How I miss getting outdoors, breathing the fresh air, feeling the sun on my face.

What can I do to bring sunlight into this season of darkness? Can I take a walk on my lunch hour, if only for twenty minutes? Can I bundle up as soon as I get home and take a stroll around the neighborhood?

*O God, I need to go outside into nature whenever I can steal a moment. It helps me feel more alive, and more connected to you if I can enjoy the beauty which you have created for us, each and every season.*

Last night our son cooked dinner. It took a long time and the kitchen was a mess, but the meal was delicious. He's always liked cooking and experimenting with food. None of the men in my family ever set foot in the kitchen, yet my son thinks he might want to be a chef.

How do I handle my teen showing an interest in something I consider atypical for his gender? When was the last time I showed an interest in something that was surprising to others?

*Loving God, show me how to remain open to all the different ways we can express ourselves. Help my teen to follow the path to what he loves even when it seems an untraditional path.*

My son didn't go to school yesterday. He decided to stay home after I left for work. This is the third time in two weeks. The school called me at work and left a message. I am furious! I feel so betrayed and ashamed!

I need to put this in perspective. I want to pursue a solution that is fair and treats both of us respectfully, but one that also acknowledges he is doing something very wrong.

Whom can I ask to help me when my anger and shame threaten to overwhelm my desire for compassion?

*Dear God, I place in your hands all the anger and shame I feel in my heart, so that I can think clearly about a solution that will best help my teen.*

This morning the air was crisp. When I took the dog for a walk, I could see his breath. The sun filtering through the trees lit up the red and green and golden leaves. There was an explosion of color all around us. At every step there was a smell, a sight, a sound, heralding that autumn had truly arrived. You couldn't help noticing. It was as if God were saying, "Pay attention. I am here. I am *everywhere*."

There is so much to notice in this season of change. What is it we need to notice that is changing in our teenager? Or what is changing in our responses to our teen?

*O God, help me to notice the miracle of you all around me. Help me notice the miracle of my teen, unfolding right in front of me.*

She came home with a terrible grade on her report card, taking no responsibility for it at all, blaming it on the teacher's inability to teach, their "personality conflict," the difficulty of the subject matter. So many excuses. I have some misgivings about this teacher, but I also know my daughter. Yet, I bit my tongue, not knowing what to say.

How can I help my daughter learn from this experience? It would be easy to blame her teacher, but I must remember that my daughter needs to accept responsibility for her part in this failure, and to explore options to make sure this doesn't happen again.

*Dear God, please help my daughter become a more responsible person. Help me to show her ways she can put her schoolwork first, and to ask for assistance if she needs it. Please, God, watch over this teacher, too, in her daily work. After all, when have I last had the courage to stand up alone in a classroom filled with* teenagers?

My son wanted to go out tonight with some of his friends. They are too old for trick-or-treating. He said that's not what they had in mind. Mischief Night is notorious for trouble making. I quizzed him about where he intended to go, and debated over whether or not I should make him stay home. He assured me that they wouldn't cause any damage. All they wanted to do was squirt shaving cream and throw "toilet paper" on a few houses. I decided to let him go, reluctantly, praying until he phoned to ask me to pick him up.

Later, he told me that some kids were destroying property, knocking over mailboxes and throwing pumpkins across the street. He said that he left that scene immediately, not wanting to get into any trouble.

If we try to protect our teens from every risky situation, they won't ever have the chance to learn valuable things about themselves, including how they will leave a situation when things start to go wrong.

*Dear God, please watch over my son as he goes out into the dark, dark night. Help him to make decisions that will keep him safe and draw him closer to your goodness.*

Halloween. My daughter wants to stay home and greet the trick-or-treaters so I can take her younger brother door-to-door. Wasn't it just last year that she dressed up like a cheerleader? Now she tells me she's much too grown up for all that. She didn't want to carve a pumpkin this year or go apple picking with us.

Holiday traditions change. Teens will often shy away from activities they think are childish, but then may complain when we neglect a tradition that they've come to count on! Making holidays full of new traditions can help keep the spirit of family alive and growing. Perhaps our teen has some other ideas about what might be fun, or they may return to these very same traditions after a year or two.

*O God, help us develop new traditions that allow us to embrace the ever-changing face of our family.*

# November

"What a marvel, what a mystery, what a joy that to be a saint is never more than a step away..."
*Rev. Michael F. Dogali*

As a child, I always believed that the saints were perfect people. It all seemed so impossible! How could one ever hope to achieve the goodness of someone like Saint Francis or Saint Bernadette? And if you couldn't be perfect, I wondered, how could you ever hope to make it to heaven?

But the saints *weren't* perfect people. Despite their human imperfections, they merely brought their passionate love for God into the world, leaving it a better place—no small task, indeed! How do I forgive myself when I'm not perfect? How do I model this self-forgiveness for my teen?

We need to help our teens strive toward perfection in their love and devotion for God, but at the same time help them to recognize that they will make mistakes along the way because it's part of being human.

*Jesus, you forgive us our sins. Please help me to forgive myself when I make mistakes. Help my teen to understand that giving their best to God, our heavenly Father, is always within their reach and "never more than a step away" if they strive for virtue and love.*

"If you're lucky, when your child is around thirty, and he has his own children, perhaps he might thank you, but don't hold your breath."

*Ron Taffel*

Should we expect gratitude? We do have a right to ask for expressions of gratitude from our teens, especially when we go out of our way to do something special for them. But genuine, heartfelt appreciation for all that we do may not happen until they are much older. As teenagers, they are usually still too egocentric to grasp the enormity of the sacrifice of parenting. And if we jump in too fast to remind them that they haven't thanked us, it deprives them of the opportunity to remember it for themselves.

*O God, help me to be patient with my teen's lack of gratitude. Show me how to foster appreciation so that he will grow into a mature, responsible, and gracious adult.*

In late autumn, it feels like everything around me is dying, everything is letting go. Of course, it's all a part of the cycle of life. The oak tree sheds her acorns so easily, tossing them to the ground by the hundreds. I wish I could let go of my teen that easily.

Autumn is a time for introspection, for contemplation of what in us needs to be discarded. What do I need to let go of, to toss aside, so that my relationship with my teen can flourish and grow?

*O God, you have seen me go through so many changes. Show me when I am holding on to the "old" way of relating to my teen. Help me to discard the old and make way for the new, as it is your desire for me to continue to move forward in my relationship with my teen.*

I had been on a business trip and came home exhausted. I missed my kids, my home, and my husband. I couldn't wait to get home, but then my teens barely said hello when I walked through the front door. And there was a huge mess waiting for me. Sometimes I wonder if it's all worth it. I'd much rather be a stay-at-home mom, with time to volunteer at the school and cart them around and clean up all their messes, but we simply can't afford it.

We all need to feel appreciated, but our teens (and spouse) don't always know how to show gratitude, or to pitch in, or they are too busy, or they "forget" that we can't do it all by ourselves.

We must model gratitude for our families and others by appreciating them *first*. But we also must expect respect and gratitude and help from our teens and spouse—just as we give it to them. Especially in two-paycheck families, we need to model appreciation and helpfulness *constantly*.

*Generous God, I praise you for all that you have given me. I am truly blessed with your love and a wonderful family. Help me to carefully examine my expectations of my teens, and my spouse, and help us to work together so that none of us has to feel overburdened.*

My daughter told me last night that two of her friends are having problems coming up with money for college. One girl is still waiting for financial aid. Her parents recently divorced and her father refuses to contribute to her education. Another girl has to get a student loan because her parents won't support her now that she's eighteen. My daughter said she never realized how lucky she was to have us support her through school!

It's a moment of grace when our teens catch a glimpse of how much we have sacrificed, and how much we love them.

*Gracious God, thank you for allowing our teen to see all we have given her. Thank you for all you have given us and continue to give us every day.*

This morning I picked up all the clothes in my son's room, made his bed, and straightened out the papers on his desk. I normally leave this chore to him, shutting the door to hide all of his messiness, but today I wanted to surprise him. We've been at odds lately, and I hoped he might appreciate the gesture.

While it's nice to be appreciated, we need to be careful about our expectations. Our teens may notice the special things we do for them—or they may not. It shouldn't stop us from doing those things, though, as it can sometimes break a negative cycle. As parents, we often will need to reach out first.

*O God, help me when I feel myself being reluctant to give to others. Remind me to give to those I love, even when I expect nothing in return.*

**Expecting nothing in return** 

My daughter offered to clean the house for me, because I was sick with the flu. When I eventually crawled downstairs, I saw that she really hadn't done such a great job. Sure, she had vacuumed, but there were still dirty dishes in the sink and crumbs under the kitchen table. A part of me was angry that she hadn't cleaned the way I would have, but I thanked her anyway—and when I did, she brightened and apologized for not doing a better job.

When was the last time I *truly* thanked my teen? She needs opportunities to give freely, without fear that I will be angry if things aren't done *my* way. Because I thanked her for what she did do (instead of immediately criticizing what she *didn't*) she felt appreciated, and was able to give even more the next time.

*Holy Spirit, help me to notice the gifts that you bring to me every day, especially those that come to me unexpectedly through my teen.*

"I just have to have it! It'll look so cool. Please, you don't understand how important this is!!"

How do we answer the demands of this materialistic world? Do our teens feel the need to compete with others for the latest, most "in" gadget or brand name article of clothing? In such an affluent society, it can be difficult to say no. We rationalize our overconsumption in many ways, yet when our teens have too many things, then all material things can become meaningless.

*O Lord, please help my teens learn the difference between wants and needs. Help them practice restraint in their desire for material things and to understand what is truly important.*

"O give thanks to the LORD, for he is good;
for his steadfast love endures forever."

*Psalm 107:1*

Do I remember to give thanks to God each day? Or do I dwell on my next want or perceived need? Is that bigger house or newer car or expensive pair of shoes *really* that important? There are those who are truly suffering and in great need, but we don't always remember them in our own pursuit of comfort and goods.

*O God, I praise you for all the blessings you have bestowed upon us. Help me to use these blessings to reach out to others who are in such desperate need.*

Autumn is a time for harvest, a time for enjoying the fruits of our labors and for sharing our blessings with those less fortunate

What am I harvesting in my life? What is my teen harvesting? Have I spent quality time recently with my teen, listening to and encouraging him? How is our family celebrating the harvest? Do we gather friends around us? Good times? Laughter? Love? Or do we surround ourselves with people who complain, gossip, or bring us down?

It's important during this harvest time to explore who and what we are bringing into our lives, to examine if these people and things are bringing us closer to God.

*O God, you have given my family such special gifts. Help us to use this season to harvest the good things in our lives, as you always harvest the good in us.*

**What do we harvest?**

She is experiencing an awful outbreak of acne. His hair, he says, is much too red. She thinks she's flat chested. He knows he's too thin. Will they ever be self-confident about the way they look?

Teens struggle with their appearance, especially at the middle school level when most of them are trying desperately to look like everyone else (or at least not to draw attention to themselves when they don't!). Teenaged peers can be incredibly cruel about shortcomings in appearance, making it doubly hard for the teen who looks or acts "different." As parents, we need to listen to our teens' pain, to help them in their reasonable quest to fit in, and to assure them that, over time, most of these differences won't matter as much.

*O God, please show my teen that he is perfectly wonderful just the way he is. Help him to love himself, as you love him, as you have made him in your image.*

Today someone mentioned she had already finished her holiday shopping. I haven't even started! The tempo picks up during this time of year. Stores already have their holiday decorations up, and we haven't even gotten through Thanksgiving! I want to feel happy and excited, yet I feel a sense of dread rushing toward this holiday season.

It's not too early to begin thinking about how we can make the holidays more enjoyable and relaxed this year. If the uneasiness centers around too much to do, what can we let go of this year? What do we need help with? Whom can we ask?

If the unhappiness centers on being alone, or an anticipation of turbulence within our family, what do we need to do *now* to reach out to others who can help us to manage our stress and promote harmony within our family?

*Precious God, help me to slow down as the holiday season approaches. Show me ways to celebrate this blessed season with happy expectation.*

This afternoon we had planned to rake leaves. The whole family pitched in, even our youngest. Rakes and bags in hand, the work went more quickly with all of us participating. Oh, sure, there was some grumbling at first, and it was cold outside, but once we got started, it was fun! Afterward, we came inside for a cup of hot soup and a family game.

When was the last time our family worked together on a project? Are we all so busy running to individual activities that we have forgotten how to tackle something as a group? Families can regain a sense of their own unique mission when we work together toward a common goal.

*Loving Father, help me to look for opportunities that will give my teen a sense of purpose and belonging to our family.*

"You are precious in my sight,
and honored, and I love you....
Can a woman forget her nursing child,
or show no compassion for the child of her womb?
Even these may forget,
yet I will not forget you.
See, I have inscribed you on the palms of my hands."

*Isaiah 43:4; 49:15-16*

We feel these words deeply, because they speak of a God who loves us, a parent who will never forget us, who has *shown* us over and over again how precious we are.

How do we express the depth of our love for our teens? If many of our recent interactions have turned sour, our children may begin to feel like we don't love them.

*Glorious God, help me to show my teen how precious and honored he is. Let me recognize the signs when he may not be feeling particularly beloved. Help me to show him my love, as you have shown your love for me, always and forever.*

This afternoon I stood at my doorstep and watched as the geese flew overhead. There were hundreds of them, and I could hear their majestic honking. I marvel how every autumn they know to do this; they always know when it's time to move on.

Our teenagers know that adolescence is a time of separation. Instinctively, they know that they can no longer stay children. Their bodies are growing and maturing, their minds are stretching; everything in them is telling them it's almost time to move on. We see their restless stirring, their desire to spend more time with friends, to get a job, to be out in the world experiencing it on their own.

*Protective God, watch over my teens on their miraculous journey toward adulthood, as they get ready to spread their wings. I know I need to let them go, eventually, but please keep them with me just a bit longer; and help us to trust that we will both instinctively know when it's time for them to fly.*

Thus Jesus said, "If you bring forth what is within you, what you have will save you. If you do not have that within you, what you do not have within you [will] kill you."

*Gospel of Thomas, 70*

When someone upsets us in a way that brings about a stronger reaction than the situation calls for, and when we feel ourselves judging another, we need to pay attention! By identifying this flaw in someone else, we may find ourselves face to face with a flawed part of ourselves. All is not lost! It can help to acknowledge and bring forth the part of this person that makes us want to squirm—so that we can possibly identify it in ourselves. By paying attention to this "flawed" self with equal amounts of attention and compassion, we should be able to overcome it.

*O Jesus, Light of the World, help me bring forth my sins. I need to see my transgressions clearly, so they do not elude or consume me. Help me remember that you, who have brought the light to the world, will always love me, even in my darkest hour. Show me how to come closer to the wonder of you.*

There were three murders in our community last month. This used to be a safe place to raise children. I grew up here, and so did my parents. It's all so scary! It makes me want to move to another place to protect our family.

The dark side of humanity is frightening. The swiftness with which senseless violence can devastate is truly overwhelming. It reminds us of our fragility and our inability to control so many things. It is scary as a parent to think about sending our teens into a world that holds such dangers.

*God of love and understanding, please enter the hearts of those who would do us harm and heal them with your love. Please keep my family safe as we work together to promote a more peaceful community.*

My daughter and I had another screaming match, which left us both shaking and in tears. I felt so hopeless that I ran out of the house, trying to think of what to do. Walking down the road, my thoughts started to slow down and clear, and I came up with a solution that I thought made sense.

On the way home, I saw that all of the leaves had fallen off the trees. It startled me; I've been so preoccupied with the troubles in my relationship with my teen that I've missed this entire autumn season. It made me feel so sad. Then I looked up toward the stark and empty, leafless branches and found myself smiling. Even though the leaves were gone, God revealed the stars: a promise that things would improve.

How is God speaking to me? Am I listening?

God gives us all sorts of signs, if we only notice. Sometimes God is there in the comforting words of a friend. Sometimes God shows us the majesty of his nature, right at our doorstep. And at other times, God quietly taps us on our shoulder, saying, "Yes. I hear your troubled prayers. But know this: I am with you always."

*O Glorious God, please be with me when I am feeling hopeless. Help me to notice all the ways you are with me, always by my side.*

Last night I was sitting on the couch watching a movie. My daughter, who had more or less ignored me all week, sat down on the other side. Gradually, she inched her way closer and closer until she was watching the movie with her head on my lap. I didn't say a word. I didn't even breathe! I just relished this rare moment of closeness with my changeable, lovable teen.

*Dear God, help me to remember that there will be times of closeness and times of separation, but that through it all, my teen loves and needs me. Help me to be still and patient so she will know I welcome her love, whenever she chooses to come to me.*

My son was cut from the basketball team. I felt his disappointment so keenly; it reminded me of all the dreams in my life that haven't come true. He's a good player, so I was angry, wanting to somehow fix this problem. When I started to share all of this with him, he got up abruptly saying, "You're not listening. You just don't understand!"

Do I know how to be present for my child's pain?

I need to first *listen* to my child's disappointments, not offering false reassurances or tales of my own lost dreams. No matter how helpless I feel, I need to remember that especially in times of deep disappointment, I don't need to fix anything. It's more important for him to just feel *heard*.

*O God, hear my cry. My child is in pain and needs your gracious understanding and comfort.*

My daughter and a friend came home from school this afternoon and I overheard them making fun of an overweight girl in their class. I know this girl hasn't been kind to either of them, but something in their voices made me cringe. I stopped what I was doing and asked, "What about this girl's dignity? Couldn't you reach out to someone who is so obviously in pain?"

When was the last time I judged someone by the way he or she looked or acted? When did I last take the time to question and challenge when I heard my teen being critical of someone else?

*Jesus, you are champion of the weak and downtrodden. Help me to stand up for those who are unable to defend themselves. Help my teen to recognize the worth and dignity of everyone she encounters.*

 **Everyone *has worth and dignity***

She wants to go to the movies with a group of boys and girls. It's how they "date" in middle school, with groups of peers. I'm wondering whether they will be holding hands or kissing—or whether she will feel any of those innocent stirrings that start to happen around this age.

I need to continue to dialogue with my teen about sexuality, and not frighten her or avoid the subject. She needs to be able to talk with someone to help her set limits and boundaries around her emerging sexuality, so she doesn't find herself in a compromising situation.

*O God, help my teen as she begins the discovery of herself as a person, with longings and desires apart from our family. Guide her to make decisions that are uncompromising of the values we have taught her.*

My daughter was away for the weekend on a school trip. She called me on Saturday crying. She told me how horrible it was, and how she couldn't possibly survive the weekend. I hung up the phone with a heavy heart, and I fretted and worried the entire night—I barely got any sleep. I almost got into the car three times to bring her home, although she was several hours away.

On Sunday, I drove to the school's parking lot with dread, but she emerged from the bus with a huge smile on her face. When I reminded her of how upset she sounded the other day, she replied, "Oh that? It was no big deal, really."

Sometimes our teens just need a shoulder to cry on. Like us, they need someone to listen. Once they've vented, it's easy for them to let the problem go and see their way to a solution.

*Dear God, help me not to take all of my teen's problems too much to heart. Help me to recognize that she will be able to recover and move on from much of what is unfair and cruel in the world. Remind me not to hold tighter to her problems than she does. Be with her always and watch over her.*

A New England wall runs along the entire length of our road; it looks as if it's been here for a long time. The rusty brown leaves gather in the cracks in the stone wall. Old summer vines twist up the sides in some parts, holding the stones in place. Crumbling, worn rocks tumble to the ground. Yet, other sections are neat and tidy, almost *too* perfect.

What walls have I put up in my relationships with my teen? My neighbors? My God? When do I show others only the more "put together" me? When do I let people in to see all my cracks and crumbly parts?

When we allow others to truly know us, we become more intimate, more genuine, and able to be beloved.

*O God, help me to move away from my false self and toward authenticity in my relationships with my family, my friends, and especially with you.*

My son has a new friend coming for dinner, one who practices a different religion than ours. He asked if we could skip our usual grace before the meal, because he didn't want to be embarrassed in front of his friend. I told him I wasn't willing to bypass our meal prayer just so that he or his friend could feel more comfortable, but now I wonder, was I being inflexible?

When our children become teens, they really start to notice what makes their family different from others. Virtually anything our family does that is "different" can be a sudden, unexpected source of embarrassment. It's important to recognize their feelings, but not to accommodate their every whim. It can help to explain that all families are unique in rituals and traditions.

*Dear God, help us to maintain the values that we hold dear as a family. Please help my teen to take pride in his faith, and to be willing to share his love of Christ freely with others, without fear.*

"We gather together to ask the Lord's blessing."

Every year we hold an autumn gathering at our home; we call it a "harvest brunch". It is our way of reaching out to old friends and new, neighbors and relatives, before the busy holiday season begins. Instead of hostess gifts, we ask our guests if they would consider bringing a canned good to donate to the local food bank.

Who is gathered around our table this Thanksgiving? Have we invited neighbors or friends to share in our bounty? Have we given generously to those who don't have enough to eat? Have we expressed our gratitude to those who need to hear our words of praise?

*Bless us, O God, during this season of Thanksgiving. Help us to maintain a spirit of gratitude every day we have together.*

This past year seems like a blur. Days flew into weeks. Weeks flew into months. Holidays can be a time to pause and reflect. When I look around our Thanksgiving table, there are a few empty places. I can't help but think of our loved ones who have died in the past year, or who, for some reason, can't be here with us today.

*O God, help me to reflect on my blessings. Keep those who can't be with us close to you, as they will remain forever in our hearts.*

There are miracles around us, if we only notice.
The hoot of an owl, an hour before dawn.
A blue heron standing steadfast in a stream.
Miracles swirl around us like a circle of leaves
chasing each other down a path.
The path leads to light.
The light, to God.

We are coming to the season of miracles. Where do I notice miracles in my life? Who shines the light on my path toward God?

*Dear God, show me your everyday miracles all around me.*

Tonight some parents compared where their high school seniors were applying to college. Prestigious college names were being thrown around, and talk about early decision, waiting lists, and deferred status filled the room. For my teen, college is still a few years off, but I couldn't help thinking: is this what we have to look forward to? Will my teen be prepared for all of this?

It's important for us to keep calm as the college application process approaches. Some parents become overly involved in making sure their teen applies to as many prestigious schools as possible, when the right fit for their teen might be somewhere entirely different. Teens need help and guidance from their parents in this decision-making, but remember: graduation from a "certain" college is not an accurate predictor of success in the real world. It's better for us to have a somewhat relaxed approach, and to encourage our teens to do most of the work.

*Dear God, help me to know that my teen is just where he needs to be right now. Take away my fear and replace it with the confidence that you have a plan for my teen that is just right for him.*

"Expectations. They will trip us up every time."
*Anonymous*

How are my expectations leading to disappointment with my teen? Sometimes it can help to lower our expectations, at least temporarily, if our child is struggling in a certain area. It's better to help our teens to set small goals for improvement, and then to back off and let them try their best.

*O God, help me to recognize when my expectations of my teen's behavior are getting in the way of having an understanding, loving relationship with my teen.*

# December

"A gift opens doors;
it gives access to the great."

*Proverbs 18:16*

It is the season of giving. When parents have demanding careers, it can be a temptation to think that we need to make up for the time we've spent working by supplying our teens with material things. They don't really want those material gifts; the gift of our time is the most important gift of all. We must give them our complete and total attention when we are with them, and expect nothing but love in return.

*All-giving God, help me to take the time to show my teen how special he is to me. Help me to discover the exquisite pleasure of giving my time to someone I love with all of my heart.*

We decided to do a volunteer project together as a family this year for the holidays. It's the first time we have ever volunteered for something not organized by our school or church. We all grumbled about having to get up early on Saturday morning, but we had to deliver meals on wheels to elderly shut-ins, and then visit with them briefly. My teens didn't want to go; they'd wanted to sleep in. I have to admit I felt a bit of anxiety about going into stranger's homes, and I wondered about who would greet us at each door.

What a joy it was to see the look of gratitude on the people we were sent to serve. They were so happy to be noticed and cared for. We all agreed it was well worth the early rising, and even our reticent teens asked when we could do it again.

Our teens need to know that what they do makes a difference in the world around them. Occasionally, we need to push them past what they think they want to do. Sometimes the experience of helping others will lead to a passion that will carry them through the rest of their life.

*Dear God, guide us toward opportunities to serve others in your name throughout the year.*

**Volunteering as a family** 

I'm overwhelmed by everything I have to do: Christmas cards, shopping, decorating, baking cookies...the list goes on and on. There just aren't enough hours in the day—or night! I don't want to exhaust myself as I usually do every year, but what choice do I have?

As our lives get busier, we just can't "do" the holiday season by ourselves, and we can end up feeling overtired and resentful if we try. We need to ask for help, and most teens want to help, though we may have to let go of our desire to control the results! We can suggest that they try out a new recipe and fix dinner for the family one night, or put them in charge of holiday decorating for an entire room. Maybe they can help address Christmas cards or watch a younger sibling while we do our chores.

*Holy Father, don't let me become too busy to celebrate the true meaning of this miraculous season. Help me to include my teens in the preparations, as we await with joy the coming of your Son, Jesus Christ.*

As I waited in a long line to buy gifts, I found myself growing frustrated and impatient, wondering how I was going to get everything done. *There's too much to do*, I thought, *I can't wait for this season to be over!*

Then, in a moment of grace, my breathing slowed and a gentle voice seemed to whisper: What about the people who have to wait in line for *everything*? In the hungriest of places of the world, children wait for the very food they need to survive, and sometimes it's only a handful of rice or a cup of broth.

Advent is the season of waiting and expectation. What am I waiting for? How do I handle an unexpected period of waiting?

Especially at this time of year, extra time spent in waiting can be a gift. We can use this time to slow down, pause, count our blessings, and say a prayer of praise and thanksgiving for all of God's gifts to us.

*Show me, Mary, Mother of God, how to wait patiently during this holy season of Advent for the coming of all things joyous and new.*

Many kids say that being part of a "blended" family around the holidays is especially hard. The loss they feel from a divorce or the death of a parent may be revisited, along with memories of times and traditions they enjoyed when their family was still together.

If we listen to our children's pain without feeling the need to rationalize our choices, we can help our teens to deal with their loss. It might help to say, "This holiday seems especially hard for you. Please tell me more about how you feel."

*O God, help me to be truly present to my teen's feelings, just as you are always present to mine.*

This afternoon our family drove to our community center for a community tree lighting ceremony. The high school band played carols and my daughter sang a solo. We had hot cocoa and bought a wreath for our front door. When the moment arrived for lighting the tree, a collective "Ahhhhh," came from the crowd. Could this tree possibly be more beautiful than last year's?

When was the last time I participated in a community event with my family? So much planning goes into these events and many people volunteer because they believe in bringing others together to experience joy and the holiday spirit.

*Dear God, help our family to take time out of our busy schedules to join our community in celebrating the joy of this season. When we all gather in your spirit, there is hope and light.*

"Joy is prayer; joy is strength; joy is love.... A joyful heart is the inevitable result of a heart burning with love."

*Mother Teresa*

Do my teens only see the part of me that is exhausted or cranky from working so hard? How do I show my joy? Do I turn on the radio and dance around the room? Do I laugh heartily and share happiness with others?

*Dear God, help me to show my teens the ways that I experience joy, so they will know that adulthood can be full and rich. When I am not feeling joyful, help me find ways to bring joy into my heart.*

Sometimes my belief in God is so strong that I can barely speak. I have no words to express it, just tears of gratitude at the enormity of God's blessings, and a faith that seems unshakable. At other times, especially during times of hardship or stress, I question and wonder if God truly loves me, if God is *really* out there after all.

During our moments of shaken faith, God waits patiently for our return—similar to our waiting for our teen to grow out of a distant, grumpy phase. Sometimes God is not as patient. He seems to bombard us with messages in the people we meet, the things we encounter, and the events that unfold. He almost shouts at us to pay attention. It seems as if God is saying to us during these times, "After all I have given you, would you still doubt my love?"

When we find ourselves doubting God's love for us, we must remain steadfast. In our devotion to our faith and love toward our children, we model God's loving persistence for all of us.

*Patient God, remind me to pay attention when I begin to doubt or become distant. I need to come closer, to believe, to thank you for all of your blessings. During this holiday season, help me to prepare your dwelling place in my heart.*

The first snowfall. How quiet and serene. The snow floats down effortlessly from the heavens. It's always difficult to believe that there are bad things in the world after the first innocent snowfall. It reminds me of the wonderful, innocent optimism of my teen. Then I can't help but worry about the evils of this world waiting to whisk away that innocence or corrupt it somehow.

We need to remember that our teen's innocence can bring a fresh approach to the ills of the world. Energy, ideas, and courage will help shape this next generation. One teen's perseverance and optimism may help her in the fight against poverty and injustice. Another teen's hard work in biochemistry may help him find a cure for disease. Our teen's innocence and our hope in their ability to change things for the better is something we need to encourage and depend upon; our future is in their hands.

*Dear God, help me to let go of the things that hold me in a negative, pessimistic place, and give me faith in the gifts of the next generation. Help our teens to float effortlessly, like snow from the heavens, toward your joy and wonder.*

This is our first holiday in this our new home. The houses in this neighborhood are decorated for the holidays: gigantic wreaths, doorways lined with holly, candles in windows, and houses full of light and celebration. Driving down my street at night, I can't help wanting to look into windows trying to catch a glimpse of these strangers' lives.

When was the last time I struck up a conversation with a stranger? Could I turn a new neighbor into a possible friend? When did I last bring the light of my faith into someone else's life?

*Holy Spirit, show me how to reach out to my neighbor. Help me to talk about my faith in ways that are meaningful to others.*

I don't have enough money to give them a nice Christmas this year. Things are so tight! Now just isn't the time to splurge—not with the threat of layoffs in the new year. I know this season isn't supposed to be about getting things, but I feel guilty and somehow not good enough. I'm afraid my kids won't understand.

The best gifts are those that come from the heart. If we explain our financial situation to our teens, they can be remarkably compassionate and creative. Families can survive and thrive in adversity, as long as they stick together in faith and love.

*O God, help us to find abundance in our love for each other as we wait for your most glorious gift to the world, your son, Jesus Christ.*

My sister's daughter doesn't want to spend any part of the holiday with her father. He has treated her miserably in the past few months, and since their divorce, he has tried to get their daughter to side with him against her mother. The pressure on my niece is intense, and she has been calling me crying every night, dreading the upcoming holiday. She's hoping I can talk to her father and convince him to let up, but I'm afraid I won't be able to hold my tongue. I'm so angry with him for ruining her Christmas!

It can be difficult to remain neutral when so many of our own feelings get in the way. We want what is best for all parties, and we don't want to see anyone hurt, but, so often, we add our own "baggage" to the equation. This man might not be able to hear about his daughter's pain through a family member, because he might suspect motives. If we believe that a situation is truly damaging to our teen, it might help to have it sorted through by an unbiased professional therapist, mediator, or pastoral counselor, someone who can offer suggestions for a compromise that preserves the integrity of all concerned.

*O God, our Father, let the light of compassion enter our family's heart, and help us to realize that behind all anger is hurt and open wounds that wait for the warming light of healing and forgiveness.*

***Healing and forgiveness*** 

Tonight we took part in one of my favorite holiday traditions: seeing the lights at a nearby historic site. The tall pine trees in the park were decorated with thousands of lights. It was magical. We each picked our favorite tree as we walked quietly through the park. Then we went to the outbuilding on the bridge over the dam. We stood inside the warm building and watched the miniature train going around and around the tracks. I could have stood there for hours! Finally, we hurried through the cold to the barn, where some carolers had gathered. We got hot cider as always—but no one wanted to sit on Santa's lap this year.

We must not let our busy schedules and other obligations keep us from carving out cherished and blessed family time during this season. It's especially important for us to expect that our teens accompany us on family outings; they may grumble, but a bigger part of them will be glad that we "made" them come along.

*O Glorious God, lead us to the unexpected places where we can find your gifts. Please help us to open our hearts to your presence always.*

When we dropped off some canned goods at our local food bank, we saw some parents with their children waiting in line. These people were dressed in soiled clothing and were obviously *so* in need. I felt sad and uncomfortable, and I could tell my teens felt uncomfortable, too. When we talked about it later, we agreed: it's hard for us to imagine having to stand in line for food.

I don't often encounter poor and hungry people in my daily life. A part of me wants to turn away—it's too depressing. Am I giving all I can give? What would it take to give just a little bit more?

*O God, please keep watch over those less fortunate than us. Help me to give all that I can give. Help me to remember that when any child goes hungry, it is your child. It is* our *child.*

"Bells, bells, bells, bells. Christmas bells are ringing."

Do I hear a bell ringing this season? What message is it ringing out for me?

What changes do I need to make in order to be ready to hear about the coming of Christ into my life? Am I taking time for reflection and prayer? Am I listening carefully to the sounds of Advent?

Chants, carols, the quiet of a morning after a snowfall: all of these things need to be heard. What do you want me to hear, O Lord?

*O God, please bring the gift of joyous sound into my life this season. I am open and ready to hear your call.*

In anticipation of holiday guests, I begin to get anxious. Will I have enough food? Will people like their gifts? How will we all get along? I want this holiday to be perfect, but so many times someone has ended up in tears!

Trying to be responsible for the "perfect" Christmas is usually a set-up for failure. Examining unrealistic expectations can help us to gain perspective. While we can't change others, perhaps we can identify the things we want to change about *ourselves* in relation to our extended family.

We can be respectful of the needs of others. We can avoid talking about other family members when they aren't around to defend themselves. We can delight in our shared history, while recognizing that change comes to every family.

*O God, help me to be respectful of the changing face of my extended family, especially during this season of joy and expectation.*

***There is no "perfect" Christmas***

## *December 17*

"For as soon as I heard the sound of your greeting, the child in my womb leaped for joy."

*Luke 1:44*

What leaps in us when we hear our teen's voice? What do we treasure about them? When was the last time we told them so? This is a season of anticipation. What wonderful things can we anticipate from our teen?

*Help me, dear Father, to love the best in my teen, to look forward to all that they are ready to become, as we anticipate with joy the coming of your Son.*

She is so excited, running around the house, making secret trips to the store, baking cookies—I think my daughter is more "into" Christmas this year than I am. She reminded me to pick up the ingredients for our gingerbread house, a project we do together every year. She's also planning a tree-trimming party with several of her friends.

As teens mature, they begin to identify the family traditions they cherish, and may come up with a few new traditions of their own! It's important to encourage this openness as they mature into giving and loving adults.

*Thank you, dear God, for the gift of my loving, giving teen. Remind me to allow her to give in her own special way, and to cherish these times of sharing with my child.*

We went to a Christmas pageant at our church today. All around us, it seemed like there were babies crying. Behind us, a man with a terrible cough was blowing his nose and sneezing constantly. In front of us, a young couple kept giggling and talking during every carol. I tried to focus on the meaning of this pageant, to feel the spiritual wonder, but with so many distractions, it was becoming very difficult. I started to get angry and resentful. *It's ruined*, I thought, *the pageant is just ruined.*

Then, in a moment of grace, I suddenly felt so much peace. All of my anger and resentment drained away. I remembered that God loves us in all of our humanness, in all of our messiness. I remembered that God was there. In all of the noise and confusion, even in my anger and resentment, in *all* of it, God was there loving me anyway.

*O wondrous God, help me to draw closer to you. When I am feeling overwhelmed, angry, or judgmental, I need you near, loving me. Remind me of your presence always and in all things.*

My son's best friend lost his brother in a car accident around this time last year. We were nervous about inviting his family to our home for the holiday, but when we did, they seemed so grateful that someone had remembered them.

We think of the holidays as family time, but for those of us who have lost family members, or whose families are experiencing difficulties or strained relationships, this can be a very stressful time. Sometimes we are afraid to reach out to others who are in pain, because we think they may see it as an intrusion, but the opposite is usually true. Everyone yearns to be included and temporarily distracted from dwelling on a loss. Giving others the gift of our presence during a difficult time can be nourishing and healing.

*Help me, O God, to reach out to others in need by praying and doing for them in the spirit of love.*

**Reaching out to those in pain**

"...But if you want the day ahead to be full of miracles, then spend some time each morning with God."
*Marianne Williamson*

How do I start each day? Racing for a cup of coffee? Trying to catch a glimpse of the news? How much better to spend the very first part of the day with God, asking God to bless me in all that I do, and also to bless all whom I love and all whom I might encounter.

*O God, help me to start each and every day mindful of you and your love.*

It was exactly what I wanted to avoid, racing around at the last minute running my errands. But of course, just when I thought I had finished everything, I thought of something else I had to do. As I headed into the crowded store, feeling grumpy and wishing I could be home doing anything else, I ran into an old friend. And suddenly, as we laughed and shared our equally harried lives, all the frustration I was feeling seemed to melt away. And suddenly the excitement of everyone rushing about was infectious; there was happiness all around us, we could feel it. And God was there, too.

*Thank you, God, for melting away my resentment and bringing me your joy in the face of a friend.*

"Keep on doing the things that you have learned and received and heard and seen in me, and the God of peace will be with you."

*Philippians 4:9*

Peace begins within us.

If our hearts and souls are not peaceful, we cannot offer peace to others. If we are do not approach our teens with a peaceful heart, what response can we really expect from them? What am I holding on to that is preventing me from being at peace with my child? What am I afraid will happen if I let go of this?

*Prince of Peace, please soften my heart and help me to let go of my anger and the resentments of the past. Give me the strength to move closer to your gift of peace.*

We planned to go to Midnight Mass on Christmas Eve. When I was growing up, every year we went to Christmas Eve services at an abbey. My mother's cousin, Abbot Melvin, was in charge of all the monks who resided there. There was something exciting about my parents whisking me off to a strange church in the middle of the cold, dark night. The monks wore vestments, and a heavy smell of incense filled the air. The service was in Latin, and we rubbed our eyes, trying to stay awake. Their voices were hypnotic as they prayed together, and we hardly understood a word, but when they sang, it was as if angels were chanting from heaven.

*Jesus, Lamb of God, thank you for giving me the appreciation, on this holiest night, of the mysterious wonders of my faith.*

The weather just didn't cooperate. We had planned to spend the morning at home opening presents and then racing around to visit our collective relatives in the afternoon. But last night's snow and ice storm has changed everything! The electricity is out and all the roads are impassable.

So instead, we spent the afternoon peacefully. The snow was actually a blessing, forcing us to relax. We opened presents slowly, played games together, and thawed some leftover turkey for dinner. In the evening, we went for a walk in the almost daylight brightness of the new snow. Later the kids remarked that it was their best Christmas ever, and we wondered how it was that we've never managed to celebrate this day in quite this way before.

*Dear God, thank you for the gift of a blessed day spent with our family, for the time we had to enjoy each other and to contemplate what we were truly celebrating on this glorious day. Help us to know that we always have the choice to spend any day with you, and to find the blessings when things don't go as* we *plan.*

It's like this every year. The day after Christmas, we throw out mounds of trash, and then we cart more things upstairs to try to find a place for it all.

What am I going to throw out this year? What old habits or ways of seeing the world are not useful to me any longer? What ways of dealing with my teen do I need to throw away, for a fresh start for next year? Where does God fit in my life? How will I develop my spiritual practices so that there is room for God in every day?

*O God, help me to eliminate the unnecessary things that clutter my mind and my life, so that there is more space for you and my family.*

Tonight was an annual neighborhood party. Everyone gathered at our neighbor's home with armfuls of their very best food for a potluck supper. The house was decorated beautifully for the holiday. Young and old were invited, but the kids who run up and down the stairs each year keep getting bigger and bigger. My teens had a wonderful time, greeting old friends and neighbors. It was so good to spend time with this warm and generous family.

When is the last time I opened up my home to friends and neighbors? Does the thought of having a party seem too daunting an effort? Perhaps I can enlist my teen and his friends for help in preparation and clean-up if it feels like too much work for me alone.

*O God, I know that I always have a seat at your table. Remind me to invite others into my home, especially during this season. Let me be a warm light for my neighbors and friends in the cold months ahead.*

Pine needles litter the floor. Ornaments and strands of lights hang a bit lopsided. There is something sad about taking down a Christmas tree, but it's time for it to go.

For me, taking down the tree signifies the end of the holiday season, when the bleakness of winter lays ahead cold, dreary, and dark. Sometimes I wish I could put the months of January and February into a box with all of those ornaments and jump ahead to springtime.

What plans can I make so that winter doesn't seem as bleak? Are their friends waiting to be visited? Can I try out a new hobby or a new winter sport? Can I volunteer? Can I explore a new place? Can I find new ways to connect with my teen in the coming months?

*Dear God, you have created a whole world for us to explore. Help me to remember that life is more enriching when I balance "being" and "doing." Help me find more time and activities to share with my family and my teen.*

"Remember diapers? Adolescence is very similar. It's a rough time. It can be very messy and often smell bad, but it's temporary. It will end."

*Michael J. Bradley Ph.D.*

Our time of raising teenagers will end. Maybe a part of us doesn't want that to happen. We really don't want it to end, because that means the beginning of a whole other set of issues: the launching of our new young adult into the world.

*O God of all creation, when I feel myself getting frustrated with the process of raising a teenager, please remind me that it* will *end.*

We are trying to make plans for New Year's Eve, but satisfying everyone's needs is difficult. Our teen wants to spend time with his friends. We want him to be with us, if just for a little while. At first tempers flared, but we've apparently learned the art of compromise—at least for now. With both sides giving in a bit, we arrived at a solution: he will spend the earlier part of the evening with us, and then meet up with friends.

*O God, help us to remember during the coming year that there is a satisfactory compromise to every situation, and that we need to learn how to listen to the voice of the Holy Spirit directing us.*

The eve of a New Year is a fresh start. Much like adolescence—the door opens and we have one foot clearly planted in front of us, while the other foot lingers, wanting to stay behind.

One of our family traditions is to review our favorite things about the year that has just passed. Then we each set a goal for the coming year. How can we hold on to the progress we've made together as a family? What have we learned that will sustain us in the months ahead? Of what accomplishment are we most proud? What are our goals for the future?

*God of newness and light, help us go forward into this New Year knowing that you are with us every day. Stay with us and guide us on this miraculous journey of life. As parents of teenagers, we have much to share with our community. Help us to continue to learn from each other and to grow. Help us to take care of ourselves when we need spiritual replenishment. Help us stay prayerfully centered and strong in our values, but compassionate to the emerging needs of our teens. And, finally, help us to do our small part to always bring your light into the world. Amen.*

# Bibliography

Bradley, Michael J. *Yes, Your Teen is Crazy!* Washington: Harbor Press, 2002.

Faber, Adele, and Elaine Mazlish. *How to Talk So Kids Can Listen*. New York: Avon Books, 1980.

Lerner, Harriet. *The Dance of Anger*. New York: Harper Collins, 1985.

McKay, Matthew, Peter D. Rogers, and Judith McKay. *When Anger Hurts*. California: New Harbinger Publications, 1989.

Morgan, John C. *Awakening the Soul*. Boston: Skinner House Books, 2001.

Natenshon, Abigail H. *When Your Child Has An Eating Disorder*. California: Jossey-Bass, 1999.

Pipher, Mary. *Reviving Ophelia*. New York: Grosset/Putnam, 1994.

Rupp, Joyce. *Praying Our Goodbyes*. Notre Dame, Indiana: Ave Maria Press, 1988.

Simmons, Rachel. *Odd Girl Out*. New York: Harcourt Books, 2002.

Taffel, Ron. *Parenting By Heart*. Boston: Addison Wesley, 1991

———. *Nurturing Good Children Now*. New York: St. Martin's Press, 1999.

Wiseman, Rosalind. *Queen Bees and Wannabes: Helping Your Daughter Survive Cliques, Gossip, Boyfriends and Other Realities of Adolescence*. New York: Crown Publishing Group, 2002.

Wolf, Anthony E. *Get Out of My Life: A Parent's Guide to the New Teenager*. New York: Farrar Straus Giroux, 1991.

***Pamela Lowell*** is a licensed clinical social worker with over twenty years of experience counseling adolescents and their families. She currently maintains a private practice specializing in self-care, stress management, addictions, eating disorders, loss and trauma. The mother of two children, she is a published poet and essayist. *Survival Meditations for Parents of Teens* is her first book

The Daughters of St. Paul operate book and media centers at the following addresses. Visit, call or write the one nearest you today, or find us on the World Wide Web, www.pauline.org

| | |
|---|---|
| **CALIFORNIA** | |
| 3908 Sepulveda Blvd, Culver City, CA 90230 | 310-397-8676 |
| 5945 Balboa Avenue, San Diego, CA 92111 | 858-565-9181 |
| 46 Geary Street, San Francisco, CA 94108 | 415-781-5180 |
| **FLORIDA** | |
| 145 S.W. 107th Avenue, Miami, FL 33174 | 305-559-6715 |
| **HAWAII** | |
| 1143 Bishop Street, Honolulu, HI 96813 | 808-521-2731 |
| Neighbor Islands call: | 866-521-2731 |
| **ILLINOIS** | |
| 172 North Michigan Avenue, Chicago, IL 60601 | 312-346-4228 |
| **LOUISIANA** | |
| 4403 Veterans Memorial Blvd, Metairie, LA 70006 | 504-887-7631 |
| **MASSACHUSETTS** | |
| 885 Providence Hwy, Dedham, MA 02026 | 781-326-5385 |
| **MISSOURI** | |
| 9804 Watson Road, St. Louis, MO 63126 | 314-965-3512 |
| **NEW JERSEY** | |
| 561 U.S. Route 1, Wick Plaza, Edison, NJ 08817 | 732-572-1200 |
| **NEW YORK** | |
| 150 East 52nd Street, New York, NY 10022 | 212-754-1110 |
| 78 Fort Place, Staten Island, NY 10301 | 718-447-5071 |
| **PENNSYLVANIA** | |
| 9171-A Roosevelt Blvd, Philadelphia, PA 19114 | 215-676-9494 |
| **SOUTH CAROLINA** | |
| 243 King Street, Charleston, SC 29401 | 843-577-0175 |
| **TENNESSEE** | |
| 4811 Poplar Avenue, Memphis, TN 38117 | 901-761-2987 |
| **TEXAS** | |
| 114 Main Plaza, San Antonio, TX 78205 | 210-224-8101 |
| **VIRGINIA** | |
| 1025 King Street, Alexandria, VA 22314 | 703-549-3806 |
| **CANADA** | |
| 3022 Dufferin Street, Toronto, ON M6B 3T5 | 416-781-9131 |
| 1155 Yonge Street, Toronto, ON M4T 1W2 | 416-934-3440 |